MW00639208

Tuna on Toast, Sister Clotildis, UFOs & Other Things I Survived

Tuna on Toast,
Sister Clotildis, UFOs
& Other Things
I Survived
Growing up in the '70s in Portland

Sherri Bobzien

Clockwise from front and center: Me, Andy, Annie, Joe, Terri,
Mitzi and Tony.

Mill City Press, Minneapolis

Copyright © 2015 by Sherri Bobzien

Mill City Press, Inc.
322 First Avenue N, 5th floor
Minneapolis, MN 55401
612.455.2293
www.millcitypublishing.com

All rights reserved. No part of this publication may be reprodu-
ced, stored in a retrieval system, or transmitted, in any form or
by any means, electronic, mechanical, photocopying, recording,
or otherwise, without the prior written permission of the author.

BIO026000 BIOGRAPHY & AUTOBIOGRAPHY / Personal
Memoirs
HUM011000 HUMOR / Marriage & Family
HUM014000 HUMOR / Religion
4.0.1.6.10.0.0   LEVEL_5   Oregon

Visit www.sherribobzien.com
Also available in e-book format.

ISBN-13: 978-1-63413-600-6
LCCN: 2015908589

Distributed by Itasca Books

Cover Design by Joe Bobzien
Typeset by Colleen Rollins

Printed in the United States of America

Dedicated to my family:
Mom, Dad, Mitzi, Terri, Tony, Joe, Annie and Andy.

Especially Joe, for making me write it.

Some of the names have been changed to protect identities.

Sister Clotildis, though, that was really her name.

Chapter One

Dad held the door as we stepped out of the cold and into the foyer of the Canton Grill. The family filed in, and my little brother and I darted under Dad's arm so we could be the first to rub the big golden Buddha in the corner. The four lanes of traffic on 82nd Avenue quieted behind us as the last kid came through and Dad let the door swing closed.

"You two, go stand next to your mother, please," Dad said to me and Andy, snapping his fingers and pointing toward Mom.

We obeyed, and my siblings and I gathered around Mom at the hostess stand. We shuffled and adjusted, trying to make room.

"Well, my goodness," the hostess said, looking east-to-west at the seven of us kids before finding Mom's eyes. "Are they all yours?"

Five seconds in and already the remarks had begun. I knew other families had a lot of kids, but not often in such rapid succession. Mom gave birth to seven children in nine years. All singles. She had exactly one menstrual cycle after she and Dad got married, and was pretty much pregnant for the next decade. What she spent on baby formula, she saved on feminine products.

"Yes, all ours!" Mom replied with the artificial cheerfulness she always displayed when asked the question, *were we all hers*. We kids had interchangeable faces—same brown eyes as Mom, identical cheeks and brows and noses, regardless of gender.

We stood quietly beside our pretty, dark-haired mother as the hostess's eyes lingered on our faces for a half second each. Her lips moved slightly and her finger jabbed at imaginary dots in the air. She looked up at Mom.

"How many?" she asked sweetly. She didn't get paid to count.

"Nine," Mom said.

The hostess looked deeply into Mom's eyes—*Are you mentally well?*—and chirped, "Of course, just a moment." She turned from us, waving a manager-type over, and after a brief whispery conversation and some synchronized staring, the hostess motioned for us to follow her through the lobby's archway and into the busy restaurant.

We trailed Mom like ducklings at a crosswalk, and I took in the sights and sounds of the dim, cavernous dining room of the Canton Grill. I loved the noise, the smells, the red booths and candles, and the furry red wallpaper. A boy tossed dishes into a plastic bin, one knee resting on the seat of a booth. Cigarette smoke wafted to the ceiling.

And the people stared.

Chow mein eaters froze mid-bite. Waitresses in white wedge tennis shoes stopped and smiled. Fathers grinned slyly at Dad; mothers sympathetically at Mom. Sisters nudged brothers.

We passed a man sitting alone at a booth; a foggy figure, veiled in blue smoke and low lighting. He straightened, rested his elbows on the table, and checked out each and every one of us kids as we passed. He tapped his cigarette against the restaurant's glass ashtray, then smiled and took a sip of his drink. He offered a nod and another smile to Dad bringing up the rear, and Dad nodded and smiled in return. We passed another table: a family of four. More smiling adults and staring children. Eyes, eyes, everywhere, eyes! We were like a float in the "Celebrating the Rhythm Method" parade! And so well-behaved it was weird. Dad had us trained. We behaved or else.

Mitzi, Terri, Tony, Joe, Annie, Andy and I scooted into the big red curvy booth in the back. We needed this booth, plus a few extra chairs; we were our own banquet. We accepted menus from the hostess, which to us kids were props. Mom and Dad would order for us, family style, and we'd get what we got, but I didn't care. I would not see, smell or taste a boiled potato tonight.

And the lecturing commenced.

"You know the rules, keep it down," Dad said, leaning in toward the center of the table until all eyes were on him. "No horsing around, no running to the bathroom every five minutes, and keep your hands to yourself. No fighting. No kicking. Put your napkin in your lap and use the fork to your right. No singing at the table. No humming, either. Don't touch that."

My anxiety was bubbling up already, anticipating the cow Dad was going to have when somebody spilled their milk. When fourteen hands are moving around a table full of delicious, exotic dishes like broccoli beef and egg foo young, milk gets spilled. I always figured Dad should have kept a dry dish towel handy at every meal, because it wasn't *if*, it was *when*.

Mom studied her menu, and as happened when we were about to part with money, her lovely, shapely lips began to disappear, receding from her face the way a frothy ocean breaker recedes from the shore. We went out to dinner about once a year because that's all we could afford, and menus made her irritated. The cost of this meal would be equal to her entire week's grocery budget, and we kids would pay for it over the next month with a few extra dinners of tuna on toast, the meal idea she got from her *Recipes from Prison* cookbook: canned tuna in a white sauce, a cup of frozen peas tossed in "for color" and extra disgustingness, warmed over and placed on toasted brown bread.

I sat between my little brother Andy and our oldest brother Tony in the booth, minding my own business, enjoying the sounds of tinkling glasses and happy diners, and perused my menu solely for the reading practice. The three of us had gotten lucky: we'd ended up at the far end of the table, away from Dad's immediate orbit. He could see us, sure, but we'd be buffered somewhat from his constant reprimands and micro-lessons on how to eat, drink, sit, gesture, blink or breathe in a restaurant.

Tony drummed his fingers on the tabletop and looked

around, bored already. Dinner out didn't excite him, plus he was faced with the possibility of enduring an entire hour without lighting anything on fire. He scanned the table for something, anything he could fiddle with, and then spotted it: the jar of mustard in the wire condiment basket, standing alongside the soy sauce and pepper sauce and other pastes and jellies of undetermined origin; the jar of mustard that looked like it hadn't been moved from this table since the day John F. Kennedy was shot.

Tony looked at me, at Andy, and back to the mustard. He leaned forward and looked down toward the end of the table, past our other siblings, at Dad.

I grabbed a sugar packet, poured it into my hand and slurped it off my palm.

"I dare you to eat a spoonful of that," Tony said to me, pointing to the mustard as I licked sugar off my skin. "Yeah, this is good stuff," he said, lifting the lid on the jar. He took his spoon and filled it with the yellow goo. Then he sniffed it, pulled back, and held the spoon in front of my face. "Try it," he said cheerfully, as if he was doing me a big favor—a real kindness—then looked away. With his right hand, he held the spoon at my mouth level, and with his left, he grabbed his menu and pretended to decide what he was going to order for dinner.

I licked my palm clean and wiped it on my pants, studying the spoonful of mustard in front of my face. I leaned forward slightly and took a whiff. It smelled like mustard (I guess), and looked like mustard (it was yellow), but I shook my head. "Nope," I said. I didn't feel like eating any mustard. Not tonight. I pushed Tony's hand away, then shot a look at Mom and Dad at the end of the booth. I didn't want to get in trouble with Dad for messing around with condiments, and Tony needed to knock it off. He risked getting in trouble for playing with the mustard, potentially wasting an entire .06 grams of food, and it was possible I would get in trouble for simply touching the spoon. Dad had said *keep your hands to yourself*, and that probably included mustard. We were doing all kinds of bad things.

Luckily, Mom and Dad were conferring with each other about our order, and not paying attention to us at the far end of the table.

Tony put the spoon back in front of my face, and Andy fidgeted in his seat, watching. Tony looked my way, nodding and gesturing with his eyes and head. His eyes and head said, "Eat it. Try it. I dare you." He seemed to enjoy insulting my intelligence, even non-verbally.

I ignored him and went back to my menu. *Why would I eat a heaping spoonful of disgusting coagulated mustard goo when I have twenty packets of sugar sitting six inches away?* I dropped my menu and grabbed another packet of C&H. I ripped it open. *Does he think I'm that stupid? That desperate for atten—*

I threw the sugar packet on the table, grabbed the spoon out of my brother's hand and shoved the whole thing in my mouth, clamping down on the entire serving, allowing each of my ten thousand taste buds, every cell of soft tissue to come in contact with this blistering sauce; this Satan's phlegm.

My eyes went wide. *What did I just put in my mouth?!* I thought it was mustard, not lighter fluid! The hottest thing I'd ever eaten was the one time Mom tried a new taco soup recipe, and this did *not* compare!

Tony and Andy watched as I began to shake my head and fan my face with my hands in an effort to stop the pain. (For the record, fanning your face? Doesn't do *squat*.) I motioned Andy for a glass of water. I was in trouble, and started to panic: Dad was going to catch us. Me. I was going to be the reason he blew up at all of us at the Canton Grill. And I was sure that if *I* got in trouble, everyone would get in trouble. That's how things worked in our family. Guilt by DNA. Dad was going to have a cow. Times seven. We were going to have a dairy farm in a minute.

My eyes shot to Dad, and I prayed he wouldn't notice my predicament: that I'd just eaten a heaping teaspoon of molten lava and my corneas were exploding out of my sockets. I was in such a state I couldn't even think to spit the stuff out. My brain was paralyzed or something. I tried to muffle my coughing while saliva and hot mustard leaked from the corners of my mouth. Luckily, Mom and Dad were still occupied at the other end of the table, pointing to the menu and talking pleasantly with the waitress while I went into convulsions—fanning and waving, drinking and fanning.

I took another shot of ice water, which dispersed the pain more evenly throughout my head: into my ears and behind my eyes, down my throat. It burned like an evil fog. Forget about Chinese water torture, try Chinese hot mustard torture. Why did this stuff exist, and why was it out on a table, for any little kid to grab hold of? It should have been locked up in a gun cabinet. My eyes puddled and my vision blurred.

"What does it taste like?" Andy said as he leaned over and put his face close to mine; his nose nearly on my cheek, as if trying to get close enough to smell the mustard, and the pain. I couldn't answer, but I think he got the message—*it tastes like flippin' fire!*—because tears were trickling out of the corners of my eyes as I leaned my head against the back of our booth. I took another drink of water and poured a sugar packet into my mouth. Even sugar didn't help.

Tony dropped his menu on the table and sat back in his seat as I lay dying. He looked around for something else to mess with—a straw to shoot spit wads, a chopstick with which to stab his neighbor—completely ignoring my discomfort. In fact, he barely cracked a smile. I'd done this for his benefit—*he'd* dared *me!*—and he didn't have the common courtesy to act the least bit impressed.

Why did I not hate him?

Finally, after sufficient water and sugar, my face recovered. I sank down into the booth, my arms splayed wide, mouth hanging open, while the world spun around me. The white spots were subsiding. I sat up and took a deep, cleansing breath.

It smelled like mustard.

I'd done it.

I had taken the dare, and survived it: kept my pain in check for the sake of my siblings.

Dinner arrived and we made it through without incident; without Dad raising his voice or popping a vein. And not one spilled milk.

* * *

As we were wrapping up our meal, reading our fortunes and waiting for Dad to finish with the check, a gentleman strolled over to chat. It was the man we'd seen on the way in, the one we'd passed with the cigarette and the amber drink.

"You sure have some nice kids," he said to Dad, smiling. "Real well-behaved." Of course. Nearly every time we were out in public, a stranger made a special trip over to Mom and Dad to comment on our behavior; to tell them how "good" we were.

"Well, thank you, I really appreciate that," Dad said, nodding pleasantly, as if he were a normal, laid-back person. As if it were as natural as could be that his seven children, all under the age of 15, were somehow miraculously calm and poised even as they were surrounded by the stimulation—the noise, the food, the secondhand smoke, the unlimited sugar packets. Dad would have people believe that *his* children's inherent desire to shriek and climb and fling noodles against the wall was kept in check because that's just how they were *wired*. He had nothing to do with it.

"We're pretty lucky," Dad said. "They're good kids."

Yeah, we were good, all right; we were in fear of Dad. My tongue had been chemically burned, and I'd barely made a peep.

Chapter Two

Dad was constantly molding, shaping, guiding; he thrived on teaching his children lessons about teamwork, work ethic, and work in general. Getting your hands dirty, a job well done and all that crap.

Dad was a worker. Not a TV watcher or a book reader or a man with a discrete hobby. If he had any hobby, it was working. He worked all day at work, and when he got home, he worked some more. Always tinkering and repairing. Lazy, my father was not. He especially loved to get outside and work, and we had to join. A morning of leaf-raking was a fall ritual, and the perfect enterprise for Dad to share with us his love of productivity and the outdoors. It held all the elements of a good chore: fresh air, tools, teamwork, and boredom.

I didn't mind the raking much, mostly because I didn't

do anything. My rake was solid wood and steel, and three times my height and weight—how effective could I be? I could barely lift it. My productivity as a leaf-raker didn't matter to my German-American father, however. The point of raking leaves wasn't about the number or volume of leaves you gathered, but rather the educational opportunity: a lesson on the concept of work, wrapped in a physical task. The majority of the work was completed by Dad, but we all had to go out in the yard and swing a rake around so we got a feel for labor.

"Let's get moving!" Dad called as he walked out the back door and into the yard, dressed in his standard weekend uniform of pegged khakis and white T-shirt, ironed and tucked in. Even working outside, Dad was dapper. The top of his bald head shone in the fall sunlight, his ring of dark hair cut short. "I said let's go!" he hollered again, this time toward the house, and one by one, my brothers and sisters and I sauntered out to our big side yard, which was as deep as our entire lot. We lined up at the door of the shed in our jeans and grubby sweatshirts, and one by one, Dad handed out rakes like bowls of porridge at an orphanage. None of us could make the excuse that we couldn't work due to a shortage of lawn tools—we didn't go out to dinner but once a year, but we each had our own rake.

After as much dilly-dallying as we could get away with, my siblings and I commenced work. The oldest, Mitzi, Terri, Tony and Joe, staked out a section of lawn and began to move their rakes around. The next in line, Annie and I, followed suit and did slightly more than nothing, while the youngest, Andy, stood with his rake and did truly and absolutely nothing. When it came to work, the only thing he did on a consistent basis was go in the house to poop. Chores of any kind caused Andy to have an urgent need for a bowel movement. And good for him.

After a minute, I took a break from standing around and leaned against one of the metal poles of the grape arbor near the house. I glanced up at the kitchen window and saw Mom inside at the sink, peering out as she did the dishes. I surveyed the blue sky, the yard, and the abundance of leaves. From the back of the yard where our gigantic maple tree stood, to the split-wood fence at the front, there were leaves enough to keep the seven of us kids (read that: *Dad*) busy for an hour or so.

I was dawdling, we were all dawdling, but Dad was on a mission—hustling around the yard and breaking a sweat even though it was only fifty-five degrees. He walked to the shed and pulled out the old barrel he used every fall to burn the leaves, and rolled it to the far side of the yard by the Donaldsons' fence. All this with a cigarette dangling from his mouth.

Dragging my rake behind me, I trotted off to another corner of the yard and got to work (read that: *pole vaulting*). I jammed the rake handle hard into the ground and propelled my puny body up and out. The goal was to launch myself several inches off the ground, while avoiding stabbing myself in the neck with one of the tines. Pole vaulting was good for ten or fifteen seconds of entertainment, or until I gave myself a welt along the underside of my chin.

Meanwhile, Dad scooped up handfuls of leaves in his weathered garden gloves and dumped them in the burn barrel, all the while prattling on about fresh air, pride of homeownership, and the satisfaction of a yard free of leaves. Then he let fly with a stream of cuss words when he realized his oldest son Tony was nowhere to be seen. "Tony, get your butt out here!" he called, as he leaned down and scooped another bundle of leaves into the fire.

Tony had disappeared, practically before we'd even started. High-risk behavior, and the type of thing that could cause Dad to blow a gasket. In addition to being *not lazy*, Dad was also *not patient*, and Tony, at 13 years of age and 104 pounds, was the workhorse of our team. He was needed.

Tony reappeared from the back of the yard near the shed and jogged toward Dad. "Here!" he called out as he grabbed his rake off the ground and got back to work—conscientious all of a sudden—putting on a real raking show. He knew he'd been gone too long, three minutes at least, and needed to make up some time.

Dad continued working, absentmindedly hollering out raking tips and motivational slogans and safety reminders: "Long strokes—put some oomph into it!" "Many hands make small work!" "Be careful around the fire!" Besides Tony, who was actually doing something in order to impress Dad, the rest of my siblings and I milked the situation, pushing the limits of Dad's relative good mood. We moved around the yard at a low-to-medium speed: Mitzi and Terri, teenagers, made halfhearted attempts at looking busy, moving a rake here and there, but there was leaning to do. Fingernails to examine. Joe took a breather and adjusted his garden gloves for the fiftieth time in five minutes. Annie, off by herself, smoothed her shiny brown hair and pulled large sections of it in front of her face, gauging the length. I found Andy and started a jousting game, while Dad raked more leaves and tossed them into the barrel.

After a minute, I noticed Tony and Joe at the far edge of the yard, standing with their rakes and talking conspiratorially; nodding and looking around, at the burn barrel, at Dad, at the rest of us kids. Tony shot over to me and Andy, looking directly at us, which made me think he had something up his sleeve that was going to make one of us cry. We stopped playing in order to listen to our big brother, who we looked up to and admired.

"OK, listen up, dipwads," he said, glancing over his shoulder toward Dad. "Today's the day." He opened his jacket to reveal the one thing that would make this leaf-raking session worth attending, and the reason for his short absence earlier. Andy and I looked at the thing, then expectantly at our brother. "Be careful, got it?" he said. "Stay away from the barrel until you hear the explosion. You'll know it when you hear it, 'cause it'll sound like a freakin' bomb went off."

He locked eyes with me and Andy, ensuring we understood the gravity of his warning—the importance of compliance; of silence.

We understood. We'd seen variations of Tony's trick a time or two, not with parents around, of course, and we loved it. We had no intention of messing things up. This prank, if successful, was going to be the highlight of the day.

"We got one shot at this—*don't* tell Dad," Tony said, and with that, he turned and strode away, making a quick round in the yard to inform our other siblings of the upcoming event.

I looked around for Dad, who was in the rear of the yard near the shed, his back to the fire.

Tony picked up his rake and made a few pulls for show, then saw his opportunity. Dad had gone into the shed and

Mom had disappeared from the kitchen window. My big brother dropped his rake, strolled near the burn barrel, and with one last look behind him, reached under his jacket and pulled out the item: the improvised explosive device.

The old battered spray paint can.

The warning label clearly stated, "CONTENTS UNDER PRESSURE. HIGHLY FLAMMABLE. KEEP AWAY FROM FIRE AND FLAME." So Tony tossed it in.

No going back now. The only way that can was coming out was in jagged little pieces.

Tony speed-walked away from the fire and returned to the front of the yard and his pantomime raking, while the rest of us eyed the barrel.

It was understood: we were all to keep to the far edges of the yard, resume our pretend raking, and stand clear of the grenade. Dad returned from the back of the yard to the center of the action, and didn't seem to notice that suddenly, instead of standing around, we were all moving about in a brisk, deliberate manner, making elaborate raking motions. As minutes passed and the tension built, seven rakes whipped back and forth. We fake-raked, looking at the burn barrel, at each other, and to Tony for unspoken cues; raised eyebrows and head nods: *It's coming. Get ready. Stand away.* We stood at the perimeter of the yard as the fire grew.

Tony called Dad over to the front of the yard in order to lure him away from the burn barrel and the potential shrapnel blast. We needed to keep Dad safe. If *he* got hurt, there was a good chance Mom would make us actually finish the job.

Tony asked Dad to explain a certain raking technique:

"Dad, which way did you say was the best? Hands held high on the handle or further down? Draw the rake straight in to your body at a perpendicular angle, or in a side-to-side motion?" *Did Dad just die and go to lesson-giving heaven?* This is what he lived for: giving advice. And to his number one son? The fruit of his loins? He'd be high all day.

He began the tutorial.

I glanced toward the fire, fairly roaring now and fueled by the leaves produced from *someone's* raking, not mine—and waited. I stood. Anticipated. Fake-raked. Glanced. Stood some more. Glanced. Pole vaulted.

I braced myself.

Dad talked to Tony near the front fence. "You see, son, if you grasp the handle more toward the center of the shaft with your left hand and then pull in to your body at a forty-five degr—"

And *KA-BOOOOOM!!!*

That paint can exploded like a bomb inside the barrel of fire and sent a shockwave through the yard. All heads jerked in the same direction, and I felt the blast of it in my underfed chest. I swore I saw the air vibrate, just like in cartoons.

Dad's head snapped toward the barrel, while shouts of "*Whoa! What was that?!*" and other exclamations of feigned astonishment rang through the yard. Behind Dad's back, Andy and I squealed and laughed and jumped up and down. Dad spun around, and we froze.

Dad, Mr. Safety, walked toward the barrel. He reached it, peered down into it, and turned to face us again, perplexed. And PO'ed. His hands went to his hips, and he gazed into each of our faces—at every child of his planted at the farthest edges of the yard, as far as we could possibly be from the barrel, each of us standing idle with rakes and each staring at our father—each of us, that is, except Tony.

Tony raked.

Chapter Three

Our family was poor, but I wasn't necessarily aware of it. We always had a working car and the electricity was never shut off or anything; I only knew that we didn't get stuff.

Receiving a trinket or a toy or the occasional candy bar while we were out shopping with Mom or Dad was an extreme rarity. If one kid got something, then all had to get something, and that just didn't happen. And we dared not ask for anything. Our parents trained us: "Don't ask for anything in here" was the standard line when we entered any type of store, be it grocery, drug, fabric, hardware. Asking for something got Mom and Dad irritated, so we knew better.

I rarely got new clothes. I was the sixth of seven kids, so naturally most of my wardrobe consisted of hand-me-downs. Added to that was the fact that Mom sewed a lot of my older siblings' clothes, so what I ended up with were *homemade* hand-me-downs: low-fashion clothes with raw seams and no manufacturer label. Humiliation, compounded.

Getting something new, an unexpected treat, was always a great desire of mine. It didn't happen. One night, however, my sisters got something new, and it was big.

* * *

A gentle breeze floated through the open front door on this warm August evening as Mom cleaned up the dinner dishes and I placed a stack of 45s an inch tall on the dining room stereo, lip-syncing to some of our old records—"Purple People Eater", "Jolly Green Giant", "Hello Muddah, Hello Fadduh", "The Witch Doctor".

I was a lip-syncing fanatic, and these were the choices I had. It was either these or Dad's favorites: Boots Randolph, Herb Alpert, or the worst: the Johnny Mann Singers. This choral group covered such tunes as "The Girl from Ipanema", "I'd Like to Get to Know You", the Association's "Windy", Petula Clark's "Downtown". The Johnny Mann Singers were on par with the Lawrence Welk Singers, only less hip. You get the idea. Total crapola.

My oldest sisters Mitzi and Terri had gone to the store with Dad to get milk and bread or something, and I spent the majority of the evening dancing around the dining room, silently singing into my favorite wooden spoon. Occasionally, Annie or Andy passed through and joined me in a dance or duet, and at about 8:30, I heard our car pull into the driveway; Dad and my sisters were home.

Mitzi strolled through the front door into the living

room, tanned and tank-topped after a day of berry picking, and Terri, browner yet, followed a few steps behind.

My normally earnest sisters looked different. I couldn't quite put my finger on it, but Mitzi held her chin a little higher as she sauntered into the house. She moved her hips in an unfamiliar way. Terri sashayed to the dining room table and flipped her long brown hair off her shoulders with sass, and Terri rarely did anything with sass. My sisters were practically strutting, as much as sweet, studious Catholic girls who still wore cat-eye glasses could strut.

I took the needle off "Witch Doctor" before Dad had to tell me to, and then I noticed it: the bag. My sister Mitzi had placed a plastic bag on the table. It had something in it, and it wasn't onions.

"We got a present," Mitzi said, as Dad smiled behind her and passed through the dining room and into the kitchen.

"What do you mean, *you got a present?*" I said to my sister. This sentence did not compute.

"Dad took us to Eastport," she replied smartly.

Eastport Plaza, the little mall up on SE 82nd and Holgate, a mile or so from our house. Eastport carried a Jean Machine, a Baskin-Robbins, a shoe store called Nordstrom, and a record store called DJ's Sound City.

"What is it?" I asked.

Mitzi pulled open the top of the draw-string bag and reached in.

"Look," she said easily, like it wasn't completely mind-blowing that she and Terri had gotten something. This something was shiny. Wrapped in plastic. Unused.

It was a record.

Dad had bought my sisters a new record album.

I didn't understand. It wasn't a birthday and it wasn't Christmas. I'm not sure this album would have even been a possibility at Christmastime. At Christmas, we usually got two or three gifts apiece, and they weren't big gifts, or even very good ones. One Christmas, I'd asked for a Chrissy doll and gotten a three-pack of socks. Another year, I'd asked for an Easy-Bake Oven and received a jumbo industrial-size box of laundry detergent. About twenty pounds' worth. Real laundry detergent! Not pretend!

Birthdays were about the same. In my entire child-hood, I had exactly one birthday party where I was allowed to invite friends and classmates from school. Mom had five kids before me, so by the time I came along, she'd pretty much had it with birthdays; I was lucky to get the one. On all my other birthdays, I had a siblings-only party. This meant lots of kids, no gifts.

Mitzi pulled the album from the DJ's bag with her berry-stained hands, and Terri leaned in for another look. Neither spoke; they simply gazed at their gift. Calmly. No shrieking or screaming.

"Let me see!" I said.

I leaned into the huddle and couldn't believe my eyes. The album was brand-new, and cool. This was no "Christ-mas Don't Be Late"—this was a *K-Tel! 20 Explosive Hits!* Real songs. By real people, not chipmunks.

We walked the two steps from the dining room table to the record player.

"Put it on!" I said. What was wrong with my sisters? "Put it on!"

Mitzi handed the album cover to Terri, and took the

record by its edges to do the customary *flip-flip, flip-flip*—deciding which side would get the inaugural play. Taking her time. I pulled my thick stack of 45s off the turntable, along with the adapter thingy that allowed me to play my now incredibly lame-in-comparison records, and Mitzi placed the K-Tel on the turntable's long spindle. She set the needle down as Terri and I stood beside her.

> *A goddess on a mountain top,*
> *Was burning like a silver flame...*

We had "Venus".

By Shocking Blue.

In our house.

I grabbed the album cover from Terri and checked out the colorful design. Black, yellow, red, blue. Groovy, modern artwork, so ugly it was beautiful. I turned it over and read the list of songs and artists while "Venus" played.

"Ma Belle Amie" by the Tee Set. "Going Up the Country" by Canned Heat. "The Rapper" by the Jaggerz. "Love Grows Where My Rosemary Goes" by Edison Lighthouse.

And there it was: "In the Summertime".

Somebody gimme my spoon! I would soon be lip-syncing my butt off to some Mungo Jerry.

Canned Heat, Mungo Jerry, Shocking Blue, the Stairsteps. This was edgy stuff, especially for my strict dad, who monitored the songs we listened to and the TV shows we watched. Allowing my sisters to get this album had to have been a stretch for him. Rock-and-roll music, performed by long-haired hippies, and black people. Dad favored clarinet great Pete Fountain.

I stood near the stereo, watching the shiny record go 'round and 'round, while my sisters continued to act weird. Cool. They started to sway ever-so-slightly to the beat of "Cry Like a Baby", finally, but still acted as if coming home with something store-bought—from a real store, not the Goodwill or Value Village—was a regular occurrence for them. As if they were entitled American teen-aged girls who got stuff. They were not! It didn't make sense to me that Mitzi and Terri weren't jumping up and down like human pogo sticks and acting as amazed as I was that there was a brand-new album in our house! It must have cost five or six dollars! Four at least.

The next song started.

"We need a new needle," Mitzi said dryly. She'd been saying that for months now, that we needed a new needle. We weren't going to get a new needle! The sun was going to burn out before our family got a new needle! Who cared? The album sounded amazing!

> *Ooh, ooh child, things are gonna get easier,*
> *Ooh, ooh child, things'll get brighter.*
> *Someday, yeah!*

My sisters and I sang. We danced. Terri turned it up. Dad hollered from the kitchen for her to turn it down. *K-Tel's 20 Explosive Hits.* We had it.

Chapter Four

I woke up early Sunday morning, practically with my mouth in a circle. I'd been practicing and practicing, trying to teach myself how to whistle, and as soon as my eyes opened, I went to work. I blew and blew and blew, and just like yesterday and the day before, nothing.

I climbed out of bed and headed downstairs, still blowing. Dry like a desert wind. I walked into the bathroom, sat down, and tried some more—I had time to kill—and a sad, hollow sigh escaped my lips.

I turned on the faucet to wash my hands, working my tongue and mouth, and suddenly: sound. Melody. Kind of. It wasn't perfect, and it would be a while before I was whistling the theme from *Andy Griffith*, but it was something. I kept it up, whistling and whistling so I wouldn't lose my momentum.

I ran down the hall into Mom and Dad's room, whistling. *I can whistle!* Dad was asleep, shirtless and on his stomach, his arm draped across Mom's back.

I shook him as I whistled, but he didn't move. I shook him again, harder this time, and put my face next to his, whistling into his eyeballs; serenading him with my monotone mouth flute. Finally, his lashes fluttered and he stirred. He opened one eye and nodded. I continued whistling—whistling, whistling, whistling!—and smacked his shoulder again. He raised his head off his pillow to look at the clock on the nightstand. 5:30. He nodded again. *I get it. You can whistle. Please leave now.*

I skipped out of the bedroom, whistling.

Chapter Five

Andy and me.

We rarely ventured to the Jantzen Beach Mall; Eastport Plaza and Lloyd Center Mall were closer to home, so even making the trip across town to Jantzen Beach was new and exciting. Plus, I'd never been to the circus before.

Mom told me that morning that the circus was going to be held outside and under a tent, which I couldn't exactly imagine, but as we approached the mall parking lot from the freeway, the picture came into view: the gigantic big-top tent, stark white against the blue, cloudless sky, decorative flags flapping in the wind. It was hot and dry and breezy on circus day, and the tent stood like a mirage in the Sahara Desert. Majestic.

I put my face out the window and gazed at the sight

as Dad pulled the Rambler into the lot and parked next to the Sears.

Two performances were being held this day, and our tickets were for the second show. Andy and I couldn't wait to get in. We jumped out of the car and took off toward the tent to wait for Mom and Dad and the rest. We were some of the first in line, and as my brother and I stood near the entrance of the tent, we couldn't help but hear the happy noises inside: the unmistakably cheery sound of circus music, the cadence of the ringmaster's voice rising and falling over the applause. I turned around to look at the sparse crowd at the entrance and realized no one was monitoring the line. Security was lax, and the only thing standing between me and a preview of a live circus was a minimum-security checkpoint. A flap of canvas.

I looked at Mom and Dad—*not paying attention*—and checked my immediate area for other official-looking adults—*none, great*—so I slowly pulled back the flap to take a peek, revealing a scene I'd never before witnessed: free-standing metal bleachers encircling a ring bedded with sawdust; clowns on unicycles; wires and pulleys and a trapeze. Stands packed with people; kids cheering and parents smiling.

I smelled hay and animals and manure, and the bouncy organ music played.

My view was partially obstructed by bleachers and bodies, but I caught a sliver of the animals in the center ring—lions and tigers and prancing horses, jumping circus dogs—being led or ridden in a grand display. I was catching a glimpse of the finale!

Then it came into view, an elephant, being led through

an opening on the far side of the arena. I glanced behind me again, checking for grown-ups. I knew I was breaking the rules by watching the end of this performance when we hadn't paid; Dad had taught me that this was practically stealing, but nobody seemed to care. I returned my attention to the show and saw the elephant lumbering in, circling the center ring, carrying on its back a pretty lady in a shiny one-piece. The lady waved to the audience as she guided and steered the huge beast to the crowd's applause.

At the very end of her ride, she parked the elephant, ambled down a rope ladder and jogged to a section of bleachers packed with little kids.

She approached the first row of kids and bent down, and from my spot near the door of the tent, I saw her lips move. She spoke to a boy, who hopped from his seat and ran to the center of the ring, where the elephant waited like an idling limo. The circus lady proceeded to guide the boy toward the rope ladder hanging off the elephant's back, and he started climbing, looking over his shoulder at his parents as the audience cheered and the music blared. He reached the top of the elephant, and adjusted himself in a saddle on the animal's back.

I couldn't believe what I was seeing. A kid getting a ride on an elephant! My lifelong dream to this point had been to meet Bill Bixby, but a little slice of life had just happened, and my new dream suddenly became this: to ride an elephant at the circus. I figured today might be my one and only shot.

I turned to Mom. "A kid's getting a ride on the elephant!"

She pulled me away from the tent flap as I caught one

final glimpse of the boy, riding around to music and applause. "A kid got a ride, Mom!"

"Well, when you guys get in there, run for the front row," Mom said to me and Andy as the line of people grew behind us. "And you may as well ham it up and clap real loud. Maybe you'll get noticed by the circus people and have a shot at the elephant ride."

Did I just hear right? Was my emotionally- and financially-frugal anti-stage mother advising us to ham it up? She usually told us to keep it down. I think she secretly *wanted* one of us to get a ride on the elephant, and our money's worth out of this show. The tickets must have cost four or five bucks a pop.

Finally, people started streaming out, and Andy and I handed our tickets to an unhappy clown and shoved through the canvas door. At Mom's instruction, we raced to the very spot in the bleachers where the boy had been picked to ride the elephant a few minutes prior.

"Front row!" I said to my little brother. "I want to ride that elephant so bad!"

"Me too!" Andy said.

Mom and Dad and our siblings settled in behind us.

The arena filled and jaunty organ music began to play. The crowd hushed. A man in a black suit and top hat entered the arena. My knees bounced and my heart pumped and the lights dimmed and the show began.

And it was fantastic. Colorful stilt-walkers. Fire-breathers. Jugglers and trapeze artists and clowns throwing confetti out of mop buckets; but I had elephant fever! Tunnel vision. The only thing on my mind was the elephant, and a ride on it. The seed had been planted at the tent's flap, and Mom had watered and fertilized. *Ham it up,* she had said. I hooted and hollered and made as big a scene as I could muster before, during, and after each act.

The finale was near: the assembly of the animals, the curtain call for the four-legged stars. *The elephant ride.* First came a lineup of the small animals, dogs jumping through hoops, and a Shetland pony or two. Next came the roaring lions and high-stepping horses. The organ music played, performers smiled and waved, and everywhere you looked, small hands were in the air.

At last the arena was cleared, and again, it came into view from the far side: the elephant, decorated in a silky elephant vest and giant tiara, carrying on its back the same pretty lady who had selected the kid in the earlier show. In her sequined blue leotard—straight-backed, smiling, tights a-shimmering—she waved to the cheering crowd, searching the stands for the lucky kid who would ride the elephant. She completed a full lap of the arena.

I waved my arms and bounced up and down on the metal bleachers, trying to get her attention. "Pick me! Pick me!" I shouted, along with every other kid in our section. The lady finished her ride, parked the animal, and slid off its back and down the rope ladder. She jogged toward the bleachers, with perfect posture, a gymnast's posture, and headed right for me and Andy. I didn't take my eyes off the sequined leotard, and then suddenly, she was in front of us!

Above the organ music, she leaned down, extended her hand, and spoke.

"Do you want to ride the elephant?"

Oh.

I put my arms down. She was talking to Andy.

Andy. The cutest kid in the section, with his crooked little smile; his moppy hair and baggy jeans. He'd been cheering. He'd been adorable.

He didn't answer. The circus lady said it again, louder this time, and with another smile. "Do you want to ride the elephant?"

My little brother paused, pointed his thumb at me, and said, "Nah, let her."

What? Yes! I jumped from my seat and made a beeline for the elephant. My wish had come true! I didn't even look back at Mom or Dad for permission; I knew I had it. We were getting some bang for our buck today. A free elephant ride!

I raced into the ring, got my bearings on the first rung of the wobbly rope ladder and started to climb, knowing and loving the fact that all eyes were on me. *I got picked!* Well, sort of. I climbed and climbed, finally reaching the top of the ladder and the huge leather saddle, which sat on top of some itchy red blanket. I settled in and grabbed the saddle knob.

I gazed out at the sea of people, and without warning, the elephant lurched into motion. I wasn't prepared. I'd received no instruction! I was all of a sudden moving, riding an elephant with seemingly two speeds: "go" and "don't go." I wobbled in the saddle, strapped in in no manner whatsoever, and held on as the lady led me—us, me and the lumbering elephant—around the circus ring. I glanced out toward the bleachers, trying to locate Mom and Dad. I wanted to see their faces, maybe get some reassurance that this was an OK thing that was happening, that it would all turn out fine, but I didn't want to take my focus off the task at hand, which was not falling off this gigantic animal and tumbling twenty feet to my death. This saddle knob, my lifeline, was the size of a billiard ball. I held tighter, and with the elephant's every step, I felt the movement of its spine, and the exaggerated side-to-side dropping motion.

Bump. Bump. Bump. Bump.

I looked around the arena again, and finally gave up on finding my parents. I locked eyes with the lady below, who led with the rope. She looked up with a smile and a nod that said, "You're doing great."

I got my balance and leaned forward. I adjusted my legs in the saddle and took a deep breath. By the time the elephant had trotted halfway around the arena, I'd gained some confidence. It was as wide as a school bus, and unless it spotted a mouse and bucked like a bronco at a rodeo, I was going to survive. I let go of the saddle horn with my right hand and gave my new friend a pat on the back of its hairy neck.

I gazed out again; at the bleachers, the lights, the performers, the audience. The music blared and the crowd cheered.

I was doing this.

I was riding an elephant. I was a star.

Chapter Six

Andy (Superman!) and our neighbor Rick.

Mom took care of us and sewed our clothes and made us dinner every night and stuff; she just wasn't the type to give us a lot of attention when we got hurt. Or maimed. She simply didn't have the time. Dropping everything and attending to the endless stream of cuts, scrapes and lacerations for seven kids wasn't feasible, not when there were the chores and the cooking and the grocery shopping to do, not to mention that braided rug to finish. Our non-coddling mother didn't even keep Band-Aids in the house; she didn't want to encourage us. If we got hurt, we had to make our own Band-Aids out of Scotch tape and wads of toilet paper. I was actually jealous of the kids at school who had real Band-Aids on their fingers. And don't get me started on Curads, with their cool packaging and fun peel-aways. Those things were amazing.

We didn't get expensive antiseptic sprays or fancy salves or bandages. Never got stitches. One time Tony stepped on a rusty nail in the yard and it went clear through the side of his foot. Did he go to the doctor? Nope. Mom just squirted some A&D ointment into the wound like she was squirting putty into a hole in the wall, and sent him back outside to play. Still barefoot.

We didn't go to the doctor for routine appointments or "well-child visits." We got our required immunizations, I suppose, we must have, but we didn't go to the doctor if we had a sinus infection, or a fever, or the flu. Or strep throat, or a burst appendix, or internal hemorrhaging or whooping cough. Mom put those on par with a broken toe—they healed themselves!

We were simply not allowed to be sick. Mom trained us not to be sick. Her mothering motto was "Toughen up." You've heard the stories of the Russian orphan babies, lying in their cold wiry cribs, who become conditioned to not cry because their cries are ignored? That was us. No use in carrying on about a stage-five ear infection when it wasn't going to get you anywhere. And no faking, either. Mom was on the extreme low end of the Munchausen-by-proxy spectrum. If you went whining to her that you were sick and needed to stay home from school, well, you'd better have some vomit to prove it. Tummyache, my eye.

She didn't believe asthma was a real thing. If my mom had been Mother of the World, it's possible asthma would have ceased to exist. Mom would have eradicated asthma by paying it no attention. In her opinion, the cause of asthma was too much maternal coddling. Spoiled kids got asthma. None of us kids had asthma; we weren't allowed.

None of us even broke a bone growing up. If we had broken a bone, Mom would have just made a homemade splint out of a branch or a wooden spoon or something, so really, what was the point? It's remarkable, but we just never went to the doctor.

Well, almost never.

* * *

Home was a two-story Old Portland style, built in the early 1900s. Six concrete steps led to our large front porch, which spanned the width of the house.

Pillars stood at the corners of the porch, and built-in seating in the form of wide ledges—backless benches—were situated between and connected to the pillars. A person could sit or stand on these waist-high ledges.

The Mitchell family lived two houses up, and Andy and little Rick Mitchell did everything together: played ball, rode bikes, threw dirt clods at the fence. The boys got together one sunny summer day for a game of Cowboys and Indians, using our porch as the setting.

Andy loved Cowboys and Indians, Cops and Robbers—any game where he got to fall, roll, or otherwise get creamed. He enjoyed yelling, *"Ohhhh, ya GOT me!"* and other phrases favored by the perishing, and could die thirty, forty times in one afternoon. He had no problem sacrificing his body by falling hard into pillars, against the house, or throwing himself onto the ground. He simply loved to croak.

The boys played, and I found a shady spot on a porch ledge to watch a nice game of shooting and dying.

It started out slowly, the Cowboys and Indians, with a little gun play—small-scale arm and shoulder wounds—maybe a thigh shot or two that caused some overemphasized limping and leg-dragging. Little Rick, with his freckles and bowl cut (picture the kid from *Mad* magazine), had a cool toy gun with a hammer that clicked with each pull of the trigger. Rick jumped all over, ducking behind Mom's flower boxes, shooting Andy from behind the pillars, clicking away to his heart's content. Andy had a gun too, and used it some, but his interest lay more in the dying than the shooting. He convulsed, swiveled, and slammed himself against surfaces, only to get up and do it all again.

The heated play went on, and eventually the sharp shooting and enthusiasm of fifteen minutes ago began to fade; the boys were getting all sweaty. The moment had come for a showdown. As I readjusted my weight on the ledge on the right side of the porch, Andy climbed onto the ledge opposite me. He hoisted himself onto his feet and stood fully upright, facing the front yard, the street, and Rick, six steps below.

Rick positioned himself at the base of the steps with his barrel trained on Andy, and blasted away with his toy gun. *Click! Click! Click! Click!* Andy stood on the ledge taking shot after shot, his arms splayed and his body twitching spastically with each pretend hit.

A shot rang out (well, clicked) and Rick the Cowboy drilled Andy the Indian. Again. For about the fiftieth time. "Die! Die! Die! You're dead!"

Andy clutched at his chest, then leaned forward, gasped dramatically, and propelled himself toward the ground eight feet below. He fell—no, he dove—like a stuntman busting through the slats of a rickety saloon balcony. Only here, there was no stuntman's mattress below to break his fall; only concrete steps, surrounded by concrete on all sides.

From my perch on the ledge, I sat upright as he hit the ground, head first.

"Andy!" I said. Ever the Method Actor, he lay motionless. This looked bad, and if he wasn't dead already, Mom was going to kill him! She was in the house, taking a much-deserved break while her children played what she thought was safely outside, and now Andy had gone and hurled himself off the porch like a loon.

I swung my legs off the ledge and ran down the steps as he rolled himself onto his back. "You're gonna be in so much trouble!" I said. "You know how Mom hates to be disturbed when she's working on the braid rug!" Andy moaned.

Then Rick and I saw it. Blood, and lots of it. Andy hopped up and performed the classic *am I bleeding* move: hand to forehead, then to eyes—forehead, eyes—and it registered. He was gushing like a geyser. I ran into the house to tell Mom, and Rick Mitchell bolted for home.

And instead of following me up the steps into the front room where Mom sat twelve feet away, Andy took off around the side of the house, sprinted down our long driveway and burst through the back door. Increasing his heart rate at this particular moment by doing a fifty-yard dash to get to Mom wasn't the greatest idea, but he was out of it. I think he might have been in shock, too—he wasn't even crying. He should have turned it on, though, because he was going to need all the sympathy he could get from our mother after leaving *this* trail of blood. He'd hit every room.

Mom sat relaxing on the couch, her perpetually

half-completed rug in her lap, when Andy came crashing into her arms. She caught him, squared his shoulders, and checked out his bloody face.

"Oh, crap," she said, as if she'd simply missed the turn into the grocery store parking lot and had to double back at the end of the block. "What did you *do*?"

"He jumped off the porch," I said. Mom exhaled and shook her head in exasperation—this rug was *never* going to get finished—and instantly, the lips disappeared. I think this time might have set a record. She stood up and dragged my bleeding brother into the kitchen. "Get off the carpet!"

By now, Joe and Annie had joined the excitement, and we all gathered around the kitchen table as Mom sat Andy down and held two fingers over the spurting hole.

Joe leaned in. "He hit an artery!" Joe didn't get worked-up about much but he was sure excited about this. Andy started to whimper.

Mom shushed everyone and took her fingers off the wound for a moment to reveal a small, triangular hole in Andy's forehead. With each passing second, each beat of his little heart, the tiny hole shot blood. And this wasn't a dribbling, or a trickling, or an oozing of blood; his forehead was spurting like a malfunctioning garden sprinkler.

Andy began to calm down. Actually, he was listing and turning pale, but the bleeding didn't seem to be slowing. Blood was still escaping through Mom's very strong fingers.

"Oh, crap," she said again, this time with some genuine worry in her voice. I think it began to dawn on her that the only way the bleeding was going to stop on this sucker was when the *heart* stopped, and that might prove too homeopathic, even for her. There would be no bandana-and-twig tourniquet today. If Dad came home tonight and there was one less kid around, there *would* be questions.

"Get me a dish towel!" she said, and Annie turned and grabbed one from the kitchen drawer. Mom pressed the towel against Andy's forehead, and held it for a moment. Slowly, the towel turned red, and we kids kept quiet. Our mother needed to think. Mom, not a screamer or a freaker-outer, was just irked, plain and simple. Her eyes scanned the kitchen, landing on the dishes in the sink, the cluttered countertop, the potatoes that needed peeling. She had things to do! And today was Saturday. Saturday was the day she cleaned the baseboards!

"Let's go," she said, and drug Andy through the dining and living rooms, toward the front door.

Joe, Annie and I followed as Mom led Andy awkwardly down the front steps, her arm wrapped around his head and the old dish towel pressed against the gushing wound. She opened the door of the Rambler, laid Andy in the passenger seat and jogged around to the driver's side.

What's going on? I wondered. *Where's she going? The hospital?*

The hospital!

Emergency! Yes! Finally! Somebody in our family was going to the hospital! Andy was bleeding to death!

We were normal!

"Tell Dad we're at Adventist!" she hollered as she started the car.

We stood together on the porch as Mom zoomed off, one hand on the steering wheel and the other holding the dish towel to Andy's head.

Annie and I plopped down onto the top step and

watched in amazement as our station wagon chugged down the street and out of sight. Joe wandered back into the house. I took a deep breath, and realized my own heart was pounding.

What a day this had been.

I wondered if Andy was going to be OK. I wondered how Mom was going to drive all the way to the hospital with just one hand. I also wondered how she was going to get the blood stains out of that dish towel. God forbid she ever threw a dish towel away.

The Mitchell boys and Andy.

Chapter Seven

I never paid much attention to how the boys did it. A dry cleaner bag, some birthday candles stuck into a crossbar made of drinking straws, and two hours later our UFO—a miniature hot air balloon, a magical flying thing—was complete. And when word spread throughout the neighborhood on a warm August evening that *a UFO was flying tonight,* the excitement grew.

Us younger kids gathered at the launch site at the end of the alley and waited. Nine o'clock. Nine-thirty. Annie and I walked along the edge of the curb, imagining we were gymnasts on a balance beam. Andy and Rick wrestled and gave each other Indian burns. The sky was darkening, and finally, with the older Mitchell brothers Dennis and Phil following behind as assistants, Tony and Joe emerged from our backyard with the UFO draped carefully over their arms.

Silently and wordlessly, the boys practically tiptoed down the grass and gravel alley. Keeping the UFO away from front doors and parents and nosy neighbors was a must—we had a real-life Mrs. Kravitz to contend with: our next-door neighbor Myrna. Myrna's sons were grown, so in the summer she spent about twelve hours a day at her front window, alternately watching her soap operas and the comings and goings of the kids on the block, her arm draped across the back of her couch. Myrna sat with her Chihuahua Peppy, and both were known to bark at kids as they passed in front of her house. Myrna, the original neighborhood watch, would have loved nothing more than to catch the 64th Street kids in the act of launching a flying fire-bag into the sky on a summer night. She made a fuss when kids so much as stepped on her grass. Then there was Dad. I didn't even like to think about what would happen if he caught us playing with fire and sending it on a trip through the air.

The launch team gathered under the tree where the alley met the street and prepped the bag for lighting. Andy and Annie and I, plus the other neighborhood kids: Rick Mitchell, Darren, James, Bob, Jimmy Shack, Butch and Joanie and Missy—surrounded them in a quiet, excited clump.

"Stand back, guys, give us some room!" Tony said.

Dennis and Phil Mitchell held the dry cleaner bag out at the top, while Tony and Joe lit the dozen candles. The boys worked quickly and intently; like three-quarter-sized NASA engineers, focused, each with his own job to do, but with a singular shared goal: Get this dry cleaner candle bag thingy heated up and in the air before Dad or Mr. Mitchell or Gladys Kravitz came down the street and busted every last one of us.

The candles burned, and we waited. We paced and hopped. After a few minutes, the bag began to glow and fill with hot air. It poofed out. Slowly. Always too slowly!

Tony held a palm under the straw-and-candle apparatus to support it, and the other boys finessed the UFO away from the tree to an open spot in the middle of the street; still cautious. Launching a UFO was a delicate matter, and there was always a chance things wouldn't work; too hot outside, too much wind, a torn bag, a defective candle-and-straw rigging.

Annie and I kept watch for unwanted grown-ups or random pedestrians.

The street was quiet, and in the distance, traffic hummed. The night had turned pure dark now, and the only things lighting our way were the street lamps, the moon, and our UFO.

Up and down the street, a few front doors were open, and squares of yellow light could be seen through the windows of nearby houses; houses filled with people having an evening snack or watching *Ironside* or *Columbo* or *McMillan & Wife*. Houses containing adults oblivious to the amazing event going on right outside their doors.

"It's clear!" Joe called. No cars on Center Street.

The boys guided the mostly-inflated UFO a few more feet as it floated and swayed and tried to fly.

"Don't let go yet," Tony said. The younger kids, ten to twelve of us now, followed behind the older boys, as instinctively and one by one, they peeled off: Joe, then Dennis, then Phil. Finally, Tony, the last one holding on, tested the readiness of our miniature hot air balloon. He placed his palm beneath the crossbar and gave a gentle, final push, propelling the glowing UFO upward.

It floated for a moment or two, then faltered. Floated and faltered. Suddenly, it rose five feet, caught a column of air and took off! It was working! It was flying! And there it went! We watched it take off, flying sideways for ten feet, then straight up for another twenty. Up and up, the UFO climbed as high as the rooftops. The audience of neighborhood kids whooped and hollered.

Go, go, go! we shouted. The UFO was airborne! Silent and airborne! Tony pumped his fist in the air and Joe raced down the street, smiling and laughing. *Yes! Yes!*

Fifteen kids chased the balloon as it rose like a leaf on an updraft. It was now forty, fifty feet high—completely out of reach and out of our control. We crossed streets diagonally trying to keep a line on it. Annie and I ran down to 65th, then to Kern Park on 66th, laughing; rooting for the UFO, and for the boys who built it.

I kept my eye on it as it flew higher—barely missing trees and wires—and marveled at the glowing piece of magic floating across the clear blue-black sky.

Spectacular.

Annie and I stopped at the far edge of the park. That was far enough for us.

We watched the UFO fly.

The older boys kept on with the chase, some on foot, some doubling up on bicycles, laughing and shouting as they disappeared down Center toward 72nd. Sometimes the UFO went way past 82nd, and the boys stayed gone for an hour or more.

When it peaked and became a small shimmering dot in the distance, Annie and I turned around and headed back. Andy and Rick and the others followed.

I always wondered how far it would go before burning out, and worried about where it would land. I also wondered what the people in the neighborhood must have thought when they saw this glowing thing flying across the sky on a hot summer evening—people who had no clue as to what it was. People had to have seen it. Drivers must have noticed. What went through their minds? It wasn't every night you saw a lit-up dry cleaner bag flying through the air.

We walked home, chatting excitedly, but I worried some more. I prayed the UFO wouldn't burn down any houses or fall onto the wires and cause a power outage. Most of all, I hoped the boys didn't get in trouble with Dad.

Chapter Eight

How I dreamed of going to the cupboard and finding a box of cookies or a carton of Ding Dongs. A bag of Doritos, Cheetos, Fritos—anything in the *-itos* family. A candy bar I didn't have to split five ways. A new chip had hit the market recently. Pringles, they were called. Potato chips packed in a tennis ball can. Genius! And super greasy. I wished Mom would get us some Pringles. She didn't.

Mom grew up on the reservation, and kids there didn't get snacks. A Sioux child living on the rez in South Dakota was raised on lunches of boiled potatoes; dinners of lard biscuits dunked in elk brine. In between, there were no snacks—there was no money for snacks. No cultural inclination. If my mom had wanted a snack, she'd have been told to go outside and find herself an acorn. This deprived childhood turned her into the mother I knew: a scrimping, saving, scratch-cooking, recycling, canning, no-snack-buying parent.

We got what she'd gotten: squat.

Mom's idea of a "snack" was saltines. "If you want a snack, make yourself some peanut butter crackers," she'd say.

Time to party, baby! Remember that commercial—the one with the good-looking teenagers, dancing and rocking out to some Bobby Sherman, passing around a sleeve of saltines? Me neither.

We didn't get any of the good stuff. No Bugles or Cheez Doodles. No Oreos or Chips Ahoy or Pop-Tarts. I dreamed, *fantasized* about chocolate Pop-Tarts; just seeing the dark brown package on the grocery store shelves made my mouth water. But we were a low-income family with seven kids. How could Mom justify buying a box of Pop-Tarts when there were only six in a box? One kid would be left out. And buying two boxes was out of the question. For one, we couldn't afford it, and two, twelve is still indivisible by seven. Here's the math: seven kids equaled no Pop-Tarts.

Once in a while, when things were flush, Mom would buy us a bag of potato chips. One bag of chips (store brand) for seven kids. When word spread that Mom had come home with the semi-annual bag of chips, things got crazy. My brothers and sisters and I raced to the kitchen, and the more aggressive of us jumped on the single bag and fought over who got to hold it until somebody ended up in tears— yet another reason Mom avoided buying chips in the first place. "You just fight over them anyway!" she said. *Well, of course we fight over them, Mom, we're starving for some saturated fats! Our skin is drying out!* We were all hovering around the twentieth percentile for weight.

Mom fed us, sure; not enough to plump us up, though, because she had a frugal trick up her sleeve. She bought foods that were technically edible, but that none of us would put into our mouths. That way, we'd never run out of food—a very strange and twisted Catch-22.

Example: puffed wheat cereal.

I guess that technically, puffed wheat was edible. But just barely. And I suppose this nasty, beige, food-like product was better than nothing, but again, just barely, because if you thought about it, puffed wheat *was* practically nothing. It had no flavor. No weight. It was like packing peanuts, except it lasted longer. We always had it in the cupboard. Because *nobody ate it.* Puffed wheat sat in our house for months before Mom would consider throwing it out.

I tried to eat it, I really did. One morning, I woke up hungry and hoping that a miracle had taken place in the night, and I'd find a box of Lucky Charms or Trix or Cocoa Puffs in the cupboard, but of course, I went to the kitchen and found the exact opposite: our heritage box of puffed wheat. The same box I'd seen up in the cupboard every day since the beginning of the school year. It was now May. This box of puffed wheat was like a cobweb. Everyone saw it, everyone wanted it gone, but nobody did anything about it.

I had no choice on this morning but to eat the puffed wheat. Almost no choice; it was puffed wheat or oatmeal. I hated both, but at least with the puffed wheat I didn't have to boil water. I hoisted myself onto the kitchen counter, and from a kneeling position, whacked the box of cereal on the high shelf until it wobbled and fell onto the counter. I dropped to the floor, and held the box at arm's length, gazing dejectedly at the low-budget picture of dried wheat turds on the front ("enlarged to show texture"—*why bother?*). I felt sorry for the poor sap whose job it was to make puffed wheat look appetizing. That was basically impossible.

I opened the box, and when I did, a strange thing happened. In nature, it might have been a beautiful thing, a firsthand, up-close illustration of the miracle of life; educational and full of wonder. In a cereal box, not so much.

A moth flew out.

I moved my face out of the way before it had the chance to fly into my gaping mouth, then closed the flaps and tossed the box back in the general vicinity of the other semi-edible food items: the ancient box of baking powder and the orphan packets of plain-wrapper gelatin. Somebody else could deal with that crap.

Heaven was spending the night with my best friend Vicki Derfler from two houses down. Vicki was an only child (no competition for snacks at her house), and walking into her mom's pantry was like walking into a convenience store: candy, cookies, pudding cups, Twinkies. My beloved Ho-Hos and Ding Dongs. Hawaiian Punch. Every snack chip and cracker imaginable. Beef jerky. Beef jerky! You may be wondering, *Was Vicki's dad a surgeon? A lawyer?* No! He was a mechanic! But the Derflers had beef jerky! Our frugal Native American mother never bought beef jerky. A shame, too: salted, dried beef—it was the food of her people!

In Vicki's freezer, ice cream was always in supply—sometimes two flavors—fresh and delicious. Mom bought us ice cream a few times, and the result was predictable: within hours of its purchase, it was ninety-five percent gone. Pounced upon. My siblings and I couldn't leisurely wait a day or two to enjoy our favorite dessert. The ice cream entered our house and we ate it when we had the chance. At the end of the evening and the ice cream dogfight, the container of leftovers, what now amounted to melted mucus, was returned to the freezer, and the crud left clinging to the sides remained for the next year or two as a goopy, discolored, coagulated goo, covered in ice crystals and freezer burn. And no matter how old, if there was anything resembling a carton of ice cream left in the freezer, we didn't dare ask Mother to buy more.

Months later, I'd be standing in the kitchen with the freezer door open, looking at the same furry carton of ice cream I remembered from before. "Mom, can we throw this ice cream out already?"

"Oh, let's keep it. There's still some left," Mom would say distractedly, sincerely, as she stood at the kitchen sink and scrubbed the dinner pans with an S.O.S pad and her bare hands.

When the cardboard packaging finally started to disintegrate, and the colors on the box began to fade with time, Mom might have thrown it out. Might have.

And the saddest thing in my childhood? It wasn't my parents' divorce, or having to change schools because of the split. It wasn't the experience of me and my siblings huddled together in the upstairs bedroom, praying—shoulders touching, heads bowed—for Mom and Dad's terrible marathon yelling and arguing to stop downstairs. The saddest thing in my childhood was powdered milk.

I'll tell you about this disgusting moo juice. It's poverty in a box: dehydrated milk flakes that when added to water make a weak, thin milk-like product. Way worse than soy milk or almond milk, any day of the week. I'm not sure this beverage is even around anymore. The state of California has probably banned it, like it has foie gras and plastic grocery bags.

If "Nothin' says lovin' like somethin' from the oven," then powdered milk says, "I kind of wish we'd have stopped at two kids."

* * *

And oh, how I wished for white bread. White bread to me signified happiness and comfort: a mother's love. Softness and palatability for delicate little mouths and tummies.

We never got it.

Mom was not about to spoil her kids by feeding them white bread. We were tough. We were Indian! We would have wheat bread! Actually, around our house we called it "brown bread." It wasn't wheat bread, which might have had some actual flavor—it was just bread that was brown. And dry. And usually stale. Sometimes Mom got our brown bread from the Franz Bread outlet store out on 102nd and Foster Road, in deep Southeast Portland. The Franz outlet sold bread that was stale to begin with, because sometimes Mom didn't have the time to let it go stale on its own. She needed to cut out the middle man.

She tried to make the stale bread more appealing by telling me that if I ate it, it would "make my hair go curly"—as if that was somehow a bonus for me. She said it often and cheerfully, generally after a culinary mishap: burnt toast, hard-cooked eggs when you'd asked for over-easy. It might have been cool to have curly hair in her day, but if it meant eating crappy food, I could do without. Plus, there was this new invention called a curling iron. I would have preferred some edible bread.

I was truly embarrassed about my school lunches. Nearly every day, I took the same thing: a sad little pressed-meat sandwich on stale, brown bread.

I always wished Mom would have at least cut the crusts off. That would have been a small improvement, and an easy fix. Four little cuts, and not much more work for her. No, that wouldn't do. What were we, spoiled?

"Did the kids on the Reservation have the crusts cut off their sandwiches?" Mom would say with a thin smile and a shake of her head as she stood at her cutting board. "I don't think so."

Well, how about a cute little triangle-shaped sandwich? Sandwiches looked so appetizing cut into triangles. Nope. Mom wouldn't dream of cutting a sandwich into triangles. That too was for spoiled kids. Crustless, triangular-shaped sandwiches made you lazy and ungrateful, obviously.

How I coveted my schoolmates' fluffy white-bread tri-angular sandwiches, lovingly placed into plastic fold-and-tuck sandwich bags. Plastic bags designed specifically for sandwiches. Carried to school in adorable right-sized paper lunch sacks.

Triangle-shaped sandwiches. Crust-free. In cute little lunch bags.

I had sandwich envy.

Mom sent me to school with my dried-out brown bread sandwich, wrapped in generic plastic wrap that had long ago lost any ability to cling, and tossed into an ugly brown paper sack left over from grocery shopping. No cute store-bought lunch sacks for us. I stood 40 inches tall and was completely dwarfed by my lunch bag—I was all out of ratio! My lunch sack looked like the kind a Depression-era kid would carry on his way to work at the sweatshop, only greasier.

This was authentic, life-shaping shame.

In the cafeteria, I held my shame and cheese sandwich on my lap and brought it to my mouth for quick bites. I tucked the gigantic dirty grocery sack under my thigh. Tried to, anyway. Even my thigh couldn't hide it.

I sat admiring the lunches of my classmates. I stole glances at Alicia Browning, sitting across and down. Alicia, with her perfect shiny blond hair and her perfect shiny lunch—her edible diorama.

She readied her beautiful meal: adorable apple slices (peeled), a six-ounce carton of whole milk, chips. She pulled her sandwich out of her pristine white (*white!*) lunch bag and placed it on her clean, restaurant-grade napkin. The sandwich was photo-ready, wrapped in wax paper that had been secured at the seam with a piece of sticky tape. What a production this sandwich was! Whose mother had the time and inclination to tape up a sandwich? My mom didn't wrap wedding gifts with this much attention.

I watched in awe as Alicia removed the sticky tape from her sandwich, and the wax paper fell gently away, like the petals of an orchid opening on a dewy morn. I ogled her roast beef on white—crust-free and cut on the diagonal, of course—and her miniature, single-serve bag of Fritos, the kind that came in a colorful multi-pack of assorted Frito-Lay products. The kind we never got.

I can't describe the emotion I felt next, but it was

stronger than envy: Alicia pulled out a Snack Pack chocolate pudding.

I couldn't even watch.

I choked down another bite of my sorry sandwich.

"When I grow up," I said to myself, "I'm going to buy my kids Snack Pack puddings. *And* little packs of Fritos. I'm going to make them white-bread sandwiches and trim the crusts off and cut them into triangles.

"I'm going to *love* my kids."

Chapter Nine

Annie and I walked the neighborhood with our canvas bag full of Thin Mints and Lemon Cremes. My skin was dry and my hair blew around, full of static. I should have worn a coat; the sun was out but it was colder than I'd expected, plus it was getting late, almost dinnertime. We needed to get home.

We walked up the steps and knocked on the door. A man answered. He was chubby and looked like he probably ate a lot of cookies; maybe we'd have some luck with him. He opened the screen door partway.

"Do you want to buy some cookies?" we asked.

"Hmmm, well, I don't know," he answered. He blocked the sun from his eyes with his left hand and stared at us as if he was waiting for more of a spiel, but *do you want to buy some cookies* was all we had. "What kind you got?" he said.

Annie reached into the bag and moved the boxes around, reciting the list of flavors.

"Well, I suppose I could buy some, if one of you wanted to give me a little kiss," he said. He looked at Annie, then me, then back to my sister.

I checked out the sweat-stained T-shirt stretched across his belly and his hairy arm holding the screen door. I turned to Annie and shook my head: *I don't want the sale that bad.* The prizes weren't even that good. My sister made a face like she'd just smelled something rotten, which she probably had. "Just come on inside and give me a little kiss," the man said to her.

Annie gave me a pained look and walked into the house with the bag. The man let the screen door slam shut, and I stayed put. I glanced around the porch, at the ceramic planters full of dirt and the paper bags stuffed with newspapers. I turned toward the street and noticed the parked cars lining both sides, the green street signs at the corner: SE 66th and Boise. I turned back to the house, and through the door I saw the man on his knees in front of Annie. He reached into the bag of cookies.

The screen door burst open and Annie rushed out of the house. "Yuck!" she said, as we ran down the steps. "He made me kiss him twice. On the lips!"

"Yuck," I said.

She handed me the money, wiped her lips, and we speed-walked home, two boxes lighter.

Chapter Ten

Dad took us camping every summer and implied that he enjoyed it, but I saw no evidence.

Camping with seven kids? Dad didn't have a lot of patience at home, when we had conveniences like running water and at least one knife that cut. Why he took us all camping—packing half our belongings into a trailer and driving seventy miles to the woods to make a separate makeshift home on a square of dirt using an antique 30-person army tent for shelter?—well, I don't have an answer.

Simply getting ready for a camping trip put Dad on a completely different anxiety level. There were too many things to remember: the gear, the lanterns, the kindling, the matches. Then the drive, so many possibilities for things to go wrong: faulty trailer lights, overheated radiators, flat tires. The vibe in the car was tense, and if we made it to the campsite without Dad or the car blowing a gasket, we were doing good.

Then we got there.

Dad hardly relaxed at all, and he couldn't stop himself from excessive cautioning. Surely one of us kids was going to chop off a leg at the shin with our camping hatchet or drown in the four-foot-wide creek. "No roughhousing near the stove! No one goes in the creek past their ankles. Watch out for that stump. Don't run with that spoon!" We'd all been walking for years now, but all of a sudden, Dad thought we didn't know how to step over a rock.

After a couple hours of trying to stay off Dad's nerves while he unpacked the gear, we had our traditional first-night-of-camping meal of spaghetti and French bread, then settled in for an evening of camping fun. Finally, darkness: time to roast marshmallows.

I stood patiently in front of Dad while he whittled sticks for us with his pocketknife and offered lessons on fire safety, twig safety, sharp point safety: "Do I need to remind you that this is not a toy?"—*whittle whittle*—"This stick could put your eye out!"

"Thanks, Dad!" I said, grabbing my roasting twig and skipping toward the fire. Dad returned to the final adjustments on our gigantic tent.

My siblings and I gathered around the fire, and a bag of fluffy white sugar blobs rested on a nearby tree stump. From the tent, Dad hollered, "Careful with those sticks, and watch your step around the fire!" Mom stood at the picnic table where she'd spend the majority of her weekend, washing dishes in a plastic tub.

I made a move to claim one of our decrepit lawn chairs

near the fire. Securing a seat of your own in our family was like a party game; we were always one or two short. It was musical chairs, with fire. I ended up slamming my bottom into a chair at the same time Mitzi did. We bonked butts, then adjusted our narrow bodies into the square foot of questionable webbing and shared the seat. I didn't care about the cramped quarters or lack of accommodation, though; I had a marshmallow on the end of a stick. I was content. Roasting marshmallows mesmerized me in a special way; I loved the calming fire, the melting marshmallow, the way mine changed colors—from white to gold to sometimes black. I gave the black ones to Mom, the woman who professed to love burnt food. I told her it'd make *her* hair go curly.

The sky above was dark and starry and the campsite, peaceful. No TV or modern distractions, just a bunch of kids sitting in wobbly lawn chairs on uneven ground, holding sharpened sticks over a roaring fire.

It's a lovely American scene—until somebody gets maimed.

I sat wedged into the tattered lawn chair alongside my oldest sister Mitzi, and together we spun our marshmallows in the flames.

Tony got up from his chair and grabbed some food from the cooler. He stood to the side of the fire, tossed a grape into the air and caught it in his mouth.

"Tony, you're going to drift into the fire!" Dad hollered from his knees as he pounded a tent stake into the ground. "Or you're going to choke on a grape! Knock it off." Dad had his back to us and somehow still sensed that Tony was messing around. In Dad's opinion, you could never be too safe. Plus, he hadn't cautioned anyone about fire safety in about three minutes. He was like an egg timer. Tony sat down, a bag of grapes in his lap and a roasting stick between his knees.

In our chair, Mitzi's arms touched mine as she laid her marshmallow torch deeper in the coals. We were quiet, gazing at the glowing fire, and good-naturedly fighting over the prime roasting real estate.

Mitzi was working up a pretty good roast on her marshmallow. Then too good a roast. "Mitz! Take it out, take it out!" I said. "Your marshmallow's on fire!"

She yanked the flaming blob out of the fire and jumped out of our chair, jostling me.

Instinct kicked in, and she began shaking her stick. She shook and shook—short, quick, up and down shakes, trying to get the fiery gob of goo to blow out. That didn't work, so she readjusted her grip and shook her stick more slowly, using exaggerated side-to-side motions; sweeping swaths of oxygen—waving the thing like an Olympic athlete waving her country's flag during Opening Ceremonies. The flame got bigger.

I kept my eyes glued to the marshmallow as she shook, until it loosened, elongated, and held to her stick by way of one last corn-syrupy thread. Finally, it came flying off the end of her torch like a comet, arcing high in the air.

I watched it fly. Then land.

On top of my hand.

Still on fire.

"Owwww!" I screamed, and jumped out of my chair. I was on fire! *My* instincts kicked in, and I began shaking my hand up and down and side-to-side, but the marshmallow wouldn't let go! It also wouldn't go out. It sat there, burning—sizzling and alive—like one of those glow snakes that we got on the 4th of July. I needed help, but just as I had been mesmerized by my own burning marshmallow a minute ago, my brothers and sisters seemed mesmerized by this one now. They all stood—or sat, if they were lucky enough to have a chair—for a good five seconds while I entertained as a human sparkler.

"Owwwwwww!" I screamed again. This was code for "help."

Mitzi dropped her stick, now marshmallow-free, and swooped in. Terri jumped up too, but neither seemed sure what to do. Dad had us practice fire drills at home, but never with marshmallows. My sisters hopped and circled around me, flapping their arms, waving at the flame, accomplishing nothing. Should they smack it with their bare hands, which could potentially hurt us all? Should they toss a wool blanket over it? Or was it flour you were supposed to throw on a marshmallow fire? Hard to remember all the rules.

Several of my brothers and sisters surrounded me now, each swiping at the flaming, moving target. I saw hands—hands, hands, hands, poking, flicking, fanning—and I shook some more, but it was useless. This thing was like sugar napalm.

"Sher burned her hand," Tony called out matter-of-factly as he sat in his chair with a bag of grapes, whittling his roasting stick to a fine symmetrical point. A little more urgency in his *Oh, by the way, your daughter's on fire* statement would have been nice, but Dad nonetheless dropped his mallet and sprinted over. He reached me in a few long strides, swearing under his breath, while Mom glanced toward the commotion and quickly finished up the last couple dishes before the suds evaporated completely. "Be right there!" she sang.

Mom and Dad reached me and rushed me from the fire to the picnic table as the marshmallow began to peter out. The family gathered around as I flopped down on the bench seat, and Dad grabbed and patted frantically at the sticky, smoldering blob, God-cursing this trip, this campsite, the marshmallow industry, lo, the advent of man-made flame. Mom handed him a dish towel and finally, mercifully, the marshmallow was extinguished.

Dad pulled the towel away, exposing pieces of marshmallow goop still attached to my mangled hand. "Oh, Jesus," he muttered, "Jesus, Jesus, Jesus," as he held my wrist steady and plucked at the warm, sticky, charred mess.

While Dad removed the last of the sludge, I stared at the quarter-sized hole on top of my right hand. The marshmallow had peeled back my skin in a nice tidy roll, exactly like the lid of a sardine can, and I no longer saw pink, healthy skin, but white, gooey, ash-flecked under-stuff. My skin was *gone*. I believe this injury is what those in the medical profession would call a "third degree burn." Second at least.

Mom leaned in for a closer look. "Oh, good, it's not too bad," she said.

What? Not too bad?

"Are you supposed to be able to see bone?" I asked, my voice quivering.

"We'll put some ice on it," Mom said.

She hurried to the cooler for some ice, ran back and placed it gently on the burnt, bony part of my hand. The shock was wearing off, and real pain was taking its place.

My brothers and sisters stood staring. "Does it hurt?" Andy asked.

"Yes. Really bad," I said. I started to cry.

Mom held the ice to my hand and Dad stood close by. I sat at the picnic table and looked around—at the empty chairs circling the fire, the fishing poles leaning against the trailer, our gargantuan tent finally set up—and felt bad that Mom or Dad might soon announce to my siblings that we'd be interrupting our fun camping trip and heading to the nearest emergency room now that I was a bona fide burn victim. I knew some families might even call off the trip and drive home after a mishap like this.

I waited for the announcement, but all I heard was crickets—literally crickets—then the clacking of roasting sticks, the crinkling of marshmallow bags, and my siblings shuffling back to the fire; bickering over who got to sit in one of the remaining excuses for lawn chairs. A seat had just opened up.

Mom and Dad tended to me and my injury at the table, but said nothing of leaving. The unspoken message was this: we would stick it out. We were camping! You didn't stop camping to go to the hospital for a little burn! We had all this food!

Mom held me on her lap for the rest of the evening, a safe distance from the fire, in the lawn chair that was the least decomposed. She stroked my hair and offered me ice and gentle words of comfort until the pain subsided enough for me to go to bed.

My brothers and sisters were allowed to sit around the fire until bedtime, while Dad stood hovering. The marshmallow roasting had definitely lost its sparkle.

Chapter Eleven

Tony.

My best friend Vicki from two houses down earned a reputation around our house for being soft. Coddled. If Vicki got hurt or fell and skinned her knee, her mom Bonni held her gently and stroked her hair, sometimes for a good three or four minutes, or until the sting of the injury subsided. If I fell and skinned my knee, Mom yelled, "Hop up! You're fine!" as she went about her daily chores.

Mrs. Derfler was lovely and nurturing and encouraged Vicki to show her emotions—to "let it out" if feelings were hurt or something was bothering her. Our mom didn't so much believe in "letting it out." In Mom's opinion, "letting it out" was New Age psychobabble. Around our house, you kept it in.

Vicki got Bactine sprayed on her scrapes; Solarcaine

applied to her mildly sunburned shoulders. Occasionally, I saw the telltale signs of dark red on Vicki's elbow or knee: the extravagant "Mercurochrome." Our mom never bought Mercurochrome. Too expensive. And unnecessary. Mom wiped our scrapes with her thumb, which she'd basted in her spit.

Vicki got Johnson's children's aspirin. Melt-in-your-mouth, candy-flavored medicine. Pez pills. She got all the good stuff.

Yes, Vicki was soft and beautiful and quick to tears, and Tony exploited this fact. He loved to pick on my orange-haired friend. She was an easy target. Brotherless. Unaggressive and trusting. Like a gentle, wounded baby deer, practically defenseless.

One bright sunny day, Vicki and I were playing in our yard, running happily in circles, pulling grass from the ground and tossing it into the air, when Tony came around and started menacing us. And by us, I mean Vicki. He smelled new meat. Tender deer meat.

He jumped in front of Vicki to block her way.

"Vicki, don't move," he said. "There's a bee in your hair!" Vicki stopped, froze, and started in with a high-pitched, wheezing/shrieking noise; the kind of noise that rattled your spine. The type of noise that caused dogs to hide under dining room tables, paws over ears. I went to Vicki to help—and to check out the bee—but I didn't see one. I was confused, and Vicki, petrified.

"Get it off, Tony! *Get it off!*" she screamed.

"Don't move! It's still there!" he said.

"Get my mom! Get my mom!" Vicki cried. Tony stood and stared—at her head, at the "bee," ignoring her request.

Go for help? Get her mom? Nobody was getting anyone's mom.

Instead, Tony bobbed and weaved in a circle around Vicki's head, giving her updates, as if following the bee's every movement.

"Oh no, it's burrowing in your hair!" he said. "It's touching your scalp! Oh, God, something's coming out of it! I think it's having a baby! Can you feel it?!"

Vicki continued shrieking, but this time, she kept the sound contained within her mouth—letting it out meant a probable sting by the bee *and* its offspring. Her lips became a thin line and her cheeks puffed out, turning nearly the color of her hair.

"Oh man, oh man! You do not want to know what's happening now! The babies are coming!" Tony said, his eyes fixed on the top of Vicki's head. When the torture became too much to bear and tears finally came to her eyes, Tony stopped cold and said, "OK, it's gone now," and turned and walked away.

Tony also had a trick up his sleeve when things got slow. A simple move: silent psychological warfare. It required no tools and no skill.

He stared at Vicki until she cried.

He jumped in front of her, caught her eye and stared with a menacing, unblinking gaze. When Vicki tried to avert her eyes or step away, Tony moved his body to block her path. He put his face five inches from hers, crossed his eyes, and stared some more, tweaking his mouth and scrunching it up to one side until he looked like an unblinking, cross-eyed freaky demon. An inbred demon. That's what it was: he looked like a cross-eyed freaky inbred demon.

"Tony, stop staring at me!" Vicki said. "Tony, stop it!"

Tony stared some more, and in a slow, devil voice, sang, "I'm not Tonyyyy. I'm Tonyyyy's evil brotherrr."

More crying. We never even told. There was no point.

Chapter Twelve

Tony and I waited in the car, our legs up on the dash, feet hanging out a window, doing anything we could to stay cool and keep our skin from touching the hot vinyl seats. We could have gone into the air-conditioned store with Mom while she did the grocery shopping, but we chose to sit in the three-thousand-pound car sauna for forty minutes.

I sat baking in the passenger seat, gazing out my window at the people walking the strip mall sidewalk in front of our car: old people entering and exiting the Rexall Drug, mothers sitting on sticky plastic chairs inside the laundromat, kids riding their bikes in front of the Thriftway where Mom was getting groceries.

The sun streamed in through the open car window as I sat in my seat, trying not to move. For one thing, I wanted to see how much of a tan line I could get on my leg in the time it took Mom to finish the shopping, and also, I was pretty much dying of heatstroke. It was about a thousand degrees.

Tony relaxed in the driver's seat, tapping his fingers on the steering wheel, staring out his window, bored as usual.

"It's hot," I groaned.

"Yep," he replied, tapping. Our conversation for the day.

My brother bent over and started rooting around on the floorboards and in the crevices of the seats—looking for what, I didn't know—but what he surfaced with were a few pennies.

He jingled the pennies around in his fist and paused, deep in thought. He placed four or five of them in a line on the dashboard.

I looked out the window again, then made another check of my tan line. I counted the moles on my thighs. Tony reached toward his feet and came up with something else this time: his magnifying glass, which, in the summer, he never left home without—because who knew when you'd be called upon to fry some ants on a sidewalk? He kept it in his sock.

Tony held the handle of his magnifying glass in his right hand, and smacked the heavy circle of glass against the palm of his left.

Smack, smack, smack.

He leaned forward in the seat and trained his magnifying glass on the pennies on the dash, moving and tilting until he created a tight solar beam. He kept the beam of light steady on each penny, spot-broiling his little copper biscuits, moving one to the next, then back again. Thirty seconds, a minute. Long enough that a faint line of smoke began to rise, dissipating at an inch height or so. The pennies sat like a teeny-tiny row of campfires.

"You're gonna burn a hole in the dashboard!" I said to my brother. Our "new" car, an old black Buick, wasn't nice—far from it. The only nice thing about it was its name: LeSabre. This embarrassing eyesore had, among other embarrassing features, a primered gray driver's side door that was never going to be anything but primered gray. Regardless of the age and condition of the Old Gray Door, I was sure Mom didn't want any additional holes in it.

Tony kept at his baking project a while longer; he was a patient person, plus there was nothing else to do. When the coins began to turn a deeper brown and he was satisfied that they'd reached the perfect temperature of 350 degrees or so, he put his magnifying glass down on the seat between us.

"Why don't you put those pennies in your mouth?" he said, looking at me for a brief moment before turning his eyes towards the grocery store.

Oh, no, I wasn't going to fall for another "why don't you put this disgusting thing in your mouth" dare. Did he think I'd forgotten the hot mustard incident? I wasn't a complete idiot.

"Uh, yeah, why don't you?" I replied with my soon-to-be-nine-year-old's razor sharp wit.

I glanced Tony's way again, at his cute, smug face, his contented smirk; then readjusted my body to keep my legs from sticking. I wished Mom would hurry up.

Tony grabbed his magnifying glass and gave his pennies another heat-up. He touched the tip of a finger to one then pulled it away, as if he'd touched the burner of a stove.

"I dare you," he said, and again, I said no.

Now, no is a funny word. A person can say no, and mean it, but sometimes the no gets lost in some subconscious murk in the recesses of a reasonable mind. I've heard it said that *no means no,* but sometimes it means, *I don't really want to but you dared me and I want to impress you and I know I have a brain but it isn't fully developed yet, so let's give it a try!*

The next thing I knew, I had four scalding hot pennies in my mouth. I scooped them off the dashboard and popped them in like a handful of M&M's.

At first, I didn't feel anything. Nothing registered. Then I felt it. Something searing. And scorching. You know how sometimes something is so hot, it almost feels cold? Well, this wasn't one of those times.

I opened my mouth to let some steam escape, then bobbled the hot coins around from side-to-side, trying to keep them off my tongue. This was impossible, and anyway, if they weren't on my tongue, they were touching the roof of my mouth, which put them closer to my brain. There was no winning.

"Oooomp, ooomp, ooomp!" I mumbled, closed-mouthed, struggling to keep it together. I felt my brother's eyes on me, but I didn't look his way. I needed to focus, prove to him that he didn't get me. I could do this! I wasn't a baby who couldn't keep a few scalding pennies in her mouth for a few seconds!

When the pennies felt like they were burning clear through, I spit them out into my hand. Now, on top of a burnt tongue and the taste of copper in my mouth, I had a bunch of filthy, saliva-soaked pennies resting in my palm.

I glared at Tony as if to say, "Are you happy now?" and I would have, but for the time being, it hurt to talk. I threw the pennies onto the floorboard of Old Gray, opened my mouth and started sucking air in and out as fast as I could, praying for some relief. But it was no use, I was surrounded by heat.

"Owwww," I moaned, leaning forward and drooling like a stupid dog.

Tony didn't say a word. He just shook his head and exhaled sharply through his nose, the universal sound for, "God, you *are* a complete idiot," and turned his attention back to the store. I swished my tongue around my mouth a few times to get some normal-flavored spit worked back up, and also to see if my tongue still functioned. I thought for a moment that I may have done some permanent damage.

Finally, Tony straightened in his seat and spoke. "Shut up, here comes Mom."

"I didn't say anything!"

Chapter Thirteen

Mom drove the boys to the theater and put the Old Gray Door in park, not far from the front doors.

"Which movie are you going to see?" she asked, eyeing the marquee through the rain and windshield wipers. Mom didn't follow movies much. "The Disney one, or the scary one?"

"Not sure," Tony said from the passenger seat.

"Yeah, not sure," Joe and Andy said from the back.

The plan was for Mom to drop the boys at the second-run theater over on Belmont to see a movie of their choosing while she went out for a while with Aunt Billie. She'd pick them up later.

Mom rooted through her purse for a piece of paper.

"OK, well, here's a note in case you need it," she said,

scribbling permission for Andy to see the horror movie. "Have fun. I'll see you at 10:30."

The boys got out, said goodbye, and slammed the doors on Old Gray.

They walked through the cold rain and into the theater, and inside, went to check out the movie posters. Which would it be: the G-rated Disney movie about a man who inherits a run-down ski resort, or the R-rated horror film everyone had been talking about? The one with the little girl.

"*Snowball Express* looks all right, I guess," Joe said to Tony, as he studied the poster depicting a cast of characters dressed in winter gear; half struggling with wonky skis and poles, the rest riding broken-down snowmobiles.

"That looks stupid," Tony said, and he turned and walked toward the ticket booth. "Two for *Exorcist*," he told the ticket seller, who took his money, no questions asked. "Andy, you're going with me."

"Wait, what?" Joe said. "Andy, how 'bout *Snowball Express*? Hold on!"

Andy shrugged, and before he or Joe knew what was happening, he was being pulled through the lobby and into *The Exorcist*, while Joe was left standing at the ticket counter, a five dollar bill in his hand.

Though slightly fazed that his eight-year-old brother had the guts to go into the R-rated horror movie, Joe bought a popcorn and soldiered on into the smaller auditorium with the other elementary school children and their parents. How much better it would have been to have Andy with him, a real-live elementary school child to act as his beard.

No matter. Joe settled into his seat, accepted the fact that he wasn't a horror movie kind of guy, not tonight anyway, and found himself chuckling at the screwball comedy. *Hey, there's Mr. Tate from* Bewitched*! And Goober Pyle!* He leaned back, threw popcorn at his mouth and watched a bunch of doofuses fake-ski down fake mountains.

Next door, the lights dimmed and *The Exorcist* started, innocently enough, with an old man digging in the desert sand. "Is it gonna get scary?" Andy whispered to Tony.

Tony stared at the screen.

Twenty minutes in, Andy pulled his feet off the floor and onto his theater chair, and dug his fingers into Tony's upper arm. He wondered if it was too late to change his mind about movies. It *was* getting scary, and as Tony sat wide-eyed in the theater auditorium, adjusting to the vulgarities and animatronics of *The Exorcist*, his little brother practically turned to stone. Andy didn't like this stuff: creepy music and bloody crucifixes and pale, gaunt priests—he got enough of that at church. He alternately covered his eyes and ears, but the movie seeped in. He couldn't escape the terrifying images of spinning heads, flying furniture, and chunky vomit. Couldn't help but listen to Regan's tortured, pitiful cries as she lay in her bed and got violently tossed around by the evil thing: "Mother! Mother, make it stop! Mother please! Mother! Mother!" *The Exorcist* engulfed him.

Like every good (and bad) Disney movie, *Snowball Express* ended after ninety-two minutes, and Joe, the reasonable brother, the analytical middle child, the one who made better choices in general, played pinball in the lobby while he waited for Tony and Andy. At last, they exited the auditorium with the rest of the shaken, drained *Exorcist* watchers. Andy was close to tears and clung to Tony's coat sleeve as they walked toward Joe, who met them halfway, whistling a peppy tune, having just watched Jody from *Family Affair* kill it in his big-screen debut.

"How was it?" Joe asked.

"Pretty bad," Tony said, raising his eyebrows and nodding.

The boys waited outside for Mom.

Mom pulled up after her night out with Aunt Billie, and chatter filled the car on the twelve-minute drive home. Andy was too traumatized to talk, but Tony gave Mom the rundown on the devil movie, going into detail about the puking scene, the bouncing mattress, Regan's goiter, the loogie she hawked into the priest's eye. Some of the sicker stuff wasn't mentioned—Mom wouldn't have allowed talk of bloody crotches or little girls ordering priests to do perverted things. Mom drank and swore a little, but she still went to church once in a while.

Joe tried to get a word in and interject a few of his observations from *Snowball Express.* "Well, there was this one scene where they took an old steam engine of some kind and converted it into a rope tow for the ski lift, and it was plausible, I guess, to a point, but really, if you think abou—"

"Andy, remember the scene where the girl grabs the dude right in the nuts?" Tony said. "I think they popped!"

Andy gave one quick shake of his head and stared out the windshield, leaning into Mom's shoulder.

Joe, calm and un-scarred by the Disney movie, and Tony, jacked up on *The Exorcist,* continued with their movie talk while Andy sat silent—completely and justifiably wigged out. Mom patted her little one's hand as she drove, and said, "Don't worry about it, honey, it was just a movie." *Just a movie?* She hadn't seen it. *The Exorcist* was not *just a movie.*

Mom and the boys arrived home, and for the rest of the evening, Andy held on to someone. Anyone. He would not be alone. It got close to bedtime, but going to bed was the last thing he wanted to do. Bed involved darkness and mattresses and chilly upstairs bedrooms. He clung to Mom while she made herself a cup of tea in the kitchen, and Tony teased him about following her around like a lap dog. "Don't be such a baby," he said, shoving Andy once in the head and walking out of the room.

"Sweetie, you're going to have to go to bed eventually," Mom said as she sipped her tea at the kitchen table. Finally, Andy could stall no longer and made his way. He said good-night to Mom and walked upstairs with Joe to the room the boys all shared. Andy got in his pajamas, and still scared to death, crawled into his lower bunk. He tried to make small talk with Joe, engaging him in conversation about happy things: baseball, camping, *Snowball Express.* Andy was definitely done with everything *Exorcist.* He never wanted to hear the word again, and thankfully, Tony wasn't around to bring it up.

A short while later, the chatting stopped, Joe fell asleep, and Andy settled down. Still, the room was dark and quiet, and that creepy, doorless closet at the top of the staircase gaped like an evil eye just outside the boys' bedroom. The window overlooking the back yard gave Andy a perfect view of the black sky through the few remaining leaves of our big maple tree. I'll go so far as to say branches cast ominous shadows into the darkened bedroom and scritch-scratched at the house. Why not.

All of a sudden, just as Andy was drifting off, his lower bunk mattress started to move—bucking up and down and side-to-side, just like Regan's bed in *The Exorcist*! Like Satan's sled! The violent movement jolted him awake. He braced himself, grabbing the edges of his mattress with his chubby little hands as the bed shook. He yelled for Mom. "Help me! Mother, please! Help me! Help me! Mother! Mother!

"MOM!!!"

Joe sat up in his bunk and peered over the side. "What's going on?!"

"Help!" Andy cried, wide-eyed and hanging on as the lower bunk rocked and rocked. "Help!"

Finally, when he could take no more and the crying started for real, the bed-shaking stopped.

"Hoo boy… that was a good one," Tony said, scooting out from under Andy's bed where he'd been hiding for the past forty-five minutes.

What patience. Tony could wait forever if it meant scaring you half to death.

He walked to his dresser to get a nightshirt, while Andy recovered, breathing hard and drying his tears.

Mom came upstairs and poked her head in the doorway, irritated. "What's going on up here?" she said.

"Nothing," Tony said, rooting around in his dresser drawer.

Tony. I swear to God.

Chapter Fourteen

Spring rolled around and I was a few months older and wiser: I'd learned that not all mustards were created equal, and also how well copper conducted heat. Andy had mostly recovered from the *Exorcist* prank and was back to sleeping through the night. April Fools' was right around the corner, and Andy and I held a meeting. Something had to be done about Tony—this was *our* year—but we knew it would take some doing.

On April Fools' Day in our family, you had to strike early—like a cobra!—before your prankee had a chance to think about what day it was. Sometimes before they were fully awake.

We were big on April Fools' pranks. Part of it had to do with our lack of money; pulling pranks didn't cost anything. We did them all: Andy and I liked the "rubber band around handle of the kitchen sink sprayer" trick; Joe did the "Vaseline on the toilet seat" trick; and Tony, the "calling Mom just after midnight on the first of April and telling her he got busted with a bottle of Mad Dog at Lents Park and needed to be picked up at juvie" trick.

We hatched a plan.

We knew Tony's routine. Every morning, he had the same thing for breakfast: Grape-Nuts. With sugar. Lots and lots of sugar.

We had one sugar shaker in the house, a thick white plastic Tupperware job, with a closeable spout at the top. This sugar shaker had been in our family for years, handed down from my grandmother to my mother. It was our heirloom sugar shaker (our family had no valuable heirlooms to be passed down, so we passed down Tupperware), well-worn from use, and covered with marks and melty dents from sitting too close to the toaster or stove. On the eve of April Fools', Andy and I emptied the sugar shaker of its regular contents and replaced it with salt.

The old "salt-in-the-sugar-shaker" trick.

Revenge of the Dipwads.

Morning came, and Andy and I got up early. We took our seats around the small glass-topped table in our kitchen with our bowls, spoons and cereal.

The sugar shaker sat on the table as usual, in all its dented glory; a symbol of long-overdue reparation. We took our time with our breakfast, stalling, waiting for Tony to show up on this bright Saturday morning.

Finally, our big brother sauntered into the kitchen, looking rumpled and cool as usual, and greeted us as he did each morning: with no greeting. Andy and I poured our milk and sat patiently, initiating no eye contact with Tony, like any other day.

He went straight to the cupboard to ready his breakfast, grabbing a bowl and the box of Grape-Nuts.

No mention of the date.

Right on track.

Tony sat down at the table and poured his Grape-Nuts, still denying our existence—*fine with me*—as Andy and I sat quietly with our Cheerios, doing without sugar for the sake of the payoff; heads down, eyes up, legs dangling from our stools. I pretended to read the back of the cereal box, biding my time. We offered no overly-eager encouragement regarding the use of the sugar. No amateurish, "Tony, Tony, do you need your SUGAR? Here's the SUGAR!!" We knew the sugar would come in due course.

The students had become the masters.

He added milk to his bowl, grabbed the shaker and began to pour: a thick, full stream of "sugar." Like a beautiful horsetail falls. We watched as he moved the shaker back and forth over the Grape-Nuts, using grand, sweeping motions, creating a dense white blanket atop the heaping mound of nuggets.

He paused to let his cereal sit for a minute or two. (You had to let Grape-Nuts soak, otherwise the roof of your mouth would be mangled all day; Grape-Nuts were like pea-gravel.) He took the box of Grape-Nuts and read a bit of the back, then stabbed absentmindedly at his breakfast, absolutely coated in salt.

He's going to fall for it.

He looked up and caught me staring, and I slowly put my eyes back to my Cheerios and pretended to read. I took a small bite of my cereal.

Do it.

Finally, Tony submerged his spoon into his bowl of cereal, loaded up, and into his trap it went: a huge spoonful of Grape-Nuts, covered in gorgeous, snowy white fluffiness. Andy and I watched it register, and his face pucker. Watched his eyes shut tight.

Snatch the pebble from my hand.

Tony, our cool big brother, always in control, aware of his surroundings and actions, a leader at home and on the playground, had just gotten got.

His face collapsed.

"Yes, yes, yes! Ha! We got you!" Andy and I said. We jumped off our stools and pointed. "We got you! WE GOT YOU! April fools!"

Tony opened his mouth and let the disgusting mixture of Grape-Nuts, milk, salt and spit drop back into his bowl. He pushed back from the table, hollering out all the good cuss words.

What a beautiful, repulsive sight it was.

"April fools!" we shouted. Andy and I hugged and danced and hopped around like kids at a powwow. "April fools!"

Tony ran to the sink and turned on the faucet. If only we'd thought to tie a rubber band around the sprayer at the kitchen sink, he would have gotten all wet, too! We weren't that sophisticated.

In between frantic attempts to shovel handfuls of water into his mouth, he cursed some more. After a final rinse and spit, he turned off the faucet and grabbed a towel from the counter to wipe his mouth. He looked our way and glared, then smiled and nodded.

Acknowledgment. At last.

We did it. We'd gotten him. And he couldn't deny it.

Chapter Fifteen

Andy and I ran barefoot, inside and out, enjoying free reign of the house and yard. We were the only kids home on this lazy summer Saturday. The oldest, Mitzi and Terri, were out, and Annie and Tony and Joe, each at a friend's.

My little brother and I played ball outside, giving each other pop flies and grounders until we'd gotten our fill, then we dropped our gloves and ran out of the yard toward the driveway. Andy picked up the Wiffle ball and bat and started tossing the ball in front of him, whacking it against the garage door over and over, and I grabbed the basketball and practiced my dribbling. Dad had taught me, and lately, would stand beside me and count how many times I bounced the ball without messing up; fifty, a hundred, a hundred and fifty times. I'd tell him later how many I did.

Soon enough, we got bored and thirsty, and ran up the back steps and into the kitchen to see what was going on with Mom and Aunt Billie.

My aunt sat with a glass of wine at the kitchen table, chatting with Mom and fanning herself with a piece of mail, her thick black hair off her shoulders in a messy knot. She'd brought a new album with her today—a duo called Delaney & Bonnie. "Never Ending Song of Love", a sweet, lilting tune, played on the stereo in the dining room.

Mom sang along to the music as she put pots and pans away in the lower cupboards. She loved to harmonize.

A head of lettuce, a bag of carrots, and a pitcher of lemonade sat on our small table in the center of the kitchen, and a two-pound package of half-frozen hamburger thawed on the countertop next to the stove. "What's for dinner?" I asked Mom as I filled a plastic cup with water at the sink. "Meatloaf," she answered, and took a sip of her wine. Meatloaf sounded good to me; Mom's meatloaf always sounded good.

"Yum, I'm staying for dinner," Aunt Billie said, and Mom smiled.

"What else?" Andy said.

"The usual," Mom said, "cooked carrots and potatoes. Salad."

Andy and I gulped down some cool water and let our plastic cups drop in the sink.

"Save your cups!" Mom called as Andy and I ran out of the kitchen, through the dining and living rooms and out the front door.

For the next half hour, we ran laps through the house—something Dad didn't allow. "In or out!" was one of his mantras. But Dad wasn't home. We played in the grass, on the sidewalk and in the driveway until the soles of our feet were slick and nearly black with dirt, then came back in again. Mom would tell me later to wash my feet before getting into bed, as usual, and as usual, I'd barely manage to get them clean.

The Delaney & Bonnie record played, Mom visited with her sister, and Andy and I played together in the summer sun.

All was calm, and all was well. Then Dad came home.

Andy and I were in the front yard playing when we saw the car coming down the street and Dad pull in front of the house. He slammed the car door and took the front steps two at a time.

It wasn't long before the shouting started inside.

From outside, Andy and I heard the muffled, angry sounds coming from the kitchen—Dad's voice, rising and fading, Mom, yelling back, and within a few minutes, all voices: Dad's, Mom's and Aunt Billie's. The sweet country-folk sounds of Delaney & Bonnie played as backdrop.

Dad was drunk. Again.

Dad's drinking had been causing more fighting between him and Mom lately, which caused more and more prayer sessions for us kids. When the fighting started, Mitzi and Terri would usher all of us, Tony and Joe included, up the staircase and into the big bedroom to pray. With just the hall light on, we'd huddle shoulder-to-shoulder in the center of the dim room, bowing our heads while the yelling continued downstairs.

Mitzi and Terri led our seven-person prayer scrum, asking God to please make our parents stop fighting. I joined in with my little-kid prayers, but kids can only pray so long before becoming bored beyond belief. Our prayers would peter out, and we'd end up turning on the lights. We'd doodle, play the Dot Game, or kneel on the floor and throw balled-up socks into the hamper, trying to ignore the horrible, ugly words being shouted downstairs.

After an hour or so, things would quiet, and Dad would call up that he and Mom were done. "It's OK to come down now, kids," he'd say, and we'd all walk hesitantly down the steps to find Dad, strained and exhausted, with his arm around Mom, in tears and leaning stiffly into his chest. Dad would give some of us hugs as if to say, "Everything's all right now." I guess the praying worked.

On this beautiful summer day, though, there would be no praying. Andy and I just stayed outside and out of Dad's way.

Sometimes he got irritated when Aunt Billie was over. He didn't care much for her. No reason, really; my aunt was a likable person, and as pretty as Rita Coolidge. But Dad didn't like it when Billie took Mom's attention away from him, and it's possible he didn't like the fact that when Mom and Billie were together, they had a good time.

But it was anyone's guess what triggered Dad's anger on this afternoon. Maybe it was because Mom was having a glass of wine, or that dinner wasn't ready. Maybe when he got home, the stapler was moved. Or the TV was left on. Someone had left the toilet seat up. Or down.

The yelling got louder.

Andy and I finally came inside. We walked quietly in the front door, tiptoed through the living and dining rooms, then hung back in the kitchen doorway and peeked around the corner. Dust particles swirled in the wide beam of sunlight that streamed through the window opposite the stove, and there were the three of them, Mom, Dad and Aunt Billie, arguing around the kitchen table. Mom's face was flushed, and Dad's hair was a mess. When Dad was sober, his hair was never a mess.

I watched as Dad pointed and shouted at Mom—his body bent slightly at the waist for emphasis, and balance. "I told you I was going to *blah blah blah*. If I told you once, I told you a thousand *blah blah blah*."

"You never said that," Mom answered. "If you would have said that, I would have *blah blah blah*."

"Leon, why don't you just calm down and *blah blah blah*," Aunt Billie said, raising her voice. "And it might be a good idea if you just left for a while!"

"Are you telling me to get out of my own house, Billie Ann?" Dad shouted.

"Would you two stop screaming at each other!" Mom said.

"Think we should go back outside?" I whispered to Andy, and Mom heard.

"See, you're scaring the kids, Leon," she said, and turned toward the stove to occupy herself, straightening a pan that didn't need to be straightened. The pot scraped over the burner and made a metal-on-metal sound.

"The kids are fine," Dad said. "Don't turn your back on me, Audrey!"

"Why don't you *get off my back!*" Mom screamed, as she whipped around and looked Dad right in the eyes. "I'm just doing my thing!"

"Well, I'm just doing *my* thing!" Dad replied, and

with that, he spotted the pitcher of lemonade on the table, wound up, and whacked it with full force at Mom, like a tennis player swinging a racket. Dad was athletic and had a great follow-through, unfortunately for Mom. The lemonade went straight into her eyes.

Her hands flew to her face.

"You asshole!" Billie said, and she rushed to Mom.

Dad took a step toward the stove, grabbed the half-frozen block of hamburger, and turned toward the kitchen window on the opposite side of the room. He readied himself, and with a pitcher's windup, heaved the meat out the window. Another great shot. A strike! The glass shattered. Dad was poetry in motion; Nolan Ryan and Jimmy Connors rolled into one—only completely wasted.

The yelling stopped. Aunt Billie's Delaney & Bonnie album played on.

My little brother and I stood in the kitchen doorway and absorbed the scene: Dad, breathing hard, rubbing his chin and neck with his hand; Mom steadying herself on our kitchen table, wiping her eyes with a towel; Billie, comforting her sister.

"Jesus Christ, Leon. Look what you did," Aunt Billie said, looking at him and shaking her head. "Look what you did."

Broken glass lay scattered all over the counter under the window, and sticky lemonade covered our white linoleum floor.

"Mom?" I said. She didn't look up.

I didn't understand. Dad was just "doing his thing"? Throwing lemonade in someone's face and chucking meat out a window was a "thing"? Was this an organized thing? I couldn't imagine that there were a lot of clubs for meat and lemonade throwers, not in 1972. Dad was a maverick.

And now the meatloaf was history—out the window— and I could say that literally. Who knew now what we'd have for dinner. Please not tuna on toast! Mom always had tuna fish, and we always had stale bread, so that nasty meal was forever lurking in the shadows.

The day was officially ruined.

Dad stood silent for a moment, looked around the room at the mess he'd made, and walked slowly through the kitchen and out the back door to assess the damage in the yard. The anger had dissipated.

Andy and I followed him out the door and around to the side yard. We didn't speak—we knew better. Outside, he approached the window and looked up at the frame while Andy and I stood behind. He'd have to fix this tonight. Even if it was summer and warm, he couldn't leave a huge gaping hole in the main floor of the house. Good thing he was handy. I wondered how late the hardware store was open on Saturdays. Dad would know.

He didn't say much as he paced back and forth under the window, checking on the damage. "Watch where you're stepping, kids," he finally said to me and Andy as we walked around barefoot in the grass. "I don't want you guys getting hurt."

Chapter Sixteen

As usual, we filed into the living room from the hall-way, youngest to oldest. When you have a bunch of kids, you're always lined up in age order. It's cuter that way.

We faced the audience—our aunts and uncles—as our oldest sister Mitzi sat down at the piano and arranged her sheet music and our littlest brother Andy hopped onto a stool next to the piano and clicked the metronome on, signaling the start of the show, because how adorable is that?

Five, six, seven, eight!

> *I saw raindrops on my window,*
> *Joy is like the rain!*
> *Laughter runs across my pane,*

Slips away and comes again.
Joy is like the rain!

Here we were again, singing for relatives. One of my most unfavorite activities. Right up there with 8 a.m. Mass on Sundays, and having to eat my one required forkful of peas at dinner.

This was Dad's deal, this singing gig. He liked to show off our "talent" by having us sing this god-awful Catholic folk song, hymn, hairshirt set to music in front of his sisters and their husbands after a Sunday supper. Just three of Dad's five sisters were at our house on this occasion, along with their unfortunate spouses. My aunts were kind, easily entertained, too, and sat smiling through our lame recital, but I really felt for my uncles. They had to endure this thing, and they weren't even blood-related!

I saw clouds upon a mountain,
Joy is like a cloud!
Sometimes silver, sometimes gray,
Always sun not far away.
Joy is like a cloud!

I was boiling to death. Even though this was Dad's production, Mom made me wear a thick scratchy dress with a matching three-quarter sleeved jacket, which I hated. I hated dresses in general, especially ones with matching three-quarter sleeved jackets, but this one cut off the circulation in my armpits.

I should have faked sick today.

Too late.

I saw Christ in wind and thunder,
Joy is tried by storm!
Christ asleep within my boat,
Whipped by wind but still afloat.
Joy is tried by storm!

What was this song trying to say? God was in the wind and thunder? He was sleeping in a boat? I couldn't picture it. My teacher Sister Bernadette Ann had taught us that God could walk on water—he could heal the blind!—why on earth would he be sleeping in the bottom of a soggy rowboat? This song made no sense to me. I'm pretty sure God wouldn't have liked it either. God had to have had some taste.

I saw raindrops on the river,
Joy is like the rain!
Bit by bit the river grows,
'Til at once it overflows.
Joy is like the rain!

To say this song was horrible was giving it too much credit. It was a melodic turd, but Dad liked it. I think he'd developed some small-scale delusions about us becoming a singing family shortly after we'd all gone to see *The Sound of Music*. I loved *The Sound of Music*, too—my first movie ever in a theater. I adored the English nanny, the singing, the marionettes, but it gave Dad ideas that his children had what it took to be a singing family. We were good enough. We were cute enough. We would take our shot at being a kid group. We'd start with "Joy is Like the Rain", and for a test audience, we'd use Aunt Millie and Uncle Cliff.

And even though Dad was delusional, there were, perhaps, a few similarities between us and the Von Trapp family: They had a lot of kids; we had a lot of kids. They were Austrian; we were part-German. The Von Trapps' dad was a strict disciplinarian; our dad threw frozen hamburger through windows when he got drunk and enraged.

> *I saw raindrops on my window,*
> *Joy is like the rain!*
> *Laughter runs across my pane,*
> *Slips away and comes again.*
> *Joy is like the rain!*

I sang, and as the song reached its end, I felt something move through me: I was slowly being filled with the Holy Spirit! And by that I mean I prayed that this song would hurry up and *flippin' end*. I think the only time I prayed with my true heart was when I wanted something Catholic-related *to be over*.

And end it did. Finally. Singing this song for relatives was sort of like church: painful, but when it was over, you realized you'd survived something.

Chapter Seventeen

There was no wondering which teacher you were going to get for third grade at Our Lady of Sorrows. The school had one classroom and one teacher per grade, and Sister Clotildis was it for third, unfortunately for all third-graders. As I walked toward the classroom on day one, I was more scared than I had ever been in my life.

I'd dreaded this moment all summer, maybe longer. I had two years under my belt at Sorrows, and I knew what I was in for. I'd seen Sister Clotildis in action; she was well-known as the meanest nun at our school, maybe in the whole city—maybe the whole country! She never smiled, she put her hands on kids, and you couldn't escape her if you tried. Sister Clotildis was everywhere: hall duty, cafeteria duty, in the bathrooms and on the playground. Omnipresent, as it were. Kind of like God, only crabbier.

The sky shone a brilliant blue and the air was crisp on that September morning, and I was dressed in my standard-issue uniform: brown plaid skirt, white blouse and brown cardigan. Look up "ugly Catholic school uniform" in the dictionary and you will see a picture of this outfit. As I opened the door to Sister Clotildis's classroom, I felt queasy. My stomachache from earlier had not gone away.

I entered the classroom alone, and found my desk. The room was as quiet as a morgue, or Mass, and my new classmates looked about the same as I probably did: ill.

I glanced around at each kid facing forward in his or her all-in-one desk, each dressed in identical brown and white. I took in the imposing classroom: the blackboard, the teacher's large wooden desk, the huge ceiling-to-floor windows that faced the residential side street, and wished this were all a bad dream. It wasn't. This was real, and there she was: Sister Clotildis, in the flesh—and lots of it. At five-foot-three and roughly eight hundred pounds, Sister Clotildis cast a girthy shadow.

We sat petrified as Sister stood before us at the front of the room, stern and unsmiling, in the outfit *she* would wear every day: a long, black nun's dress with an all-encompassing, face-swallowing nun's habit.

Remember that craft project where you took a fresh apple, peeled it, and then carved a nose and a mouth and some eyes into it? Afterward, you let it sit for two or three weeks and as it dried out, it transformed into an old, rotten, shriveled-up apple face? That's what Sister Clotildis looked like, only come to life. And with a nun's habit.

Ask any kid who survived Catholic school and they'll tell you the same thing: nuns can be scary. Most don't tolerate foolishness, misbehavior, individualism, or humor of any kind. But Clodhopper wasn't simply intolerant or humorless; she seemed to genuinely despise kids.

Her daily M.O. was to make kids feel sad and scared, regardless of age, gender, or circumstance. It seemed that if a certain amount of time went by and she hadn't yelled at or humiliated a child, an overwhelming urge came over her, a physiological need even—to find something, anything wrong with the nearest child's behavior so she could get angry. She was like a diabetic having a hypoglycemic episode, but instead of a cup of orange juice or an oatmeal cookie, she needed to humiliate a kid.

In October, Mom went into the hospital for an emergency hysterectomy. After incubating and delivering seven kids in less than a decade, her uterus finally imploded, and the nuns at Sorrows somehow knew all about it.

It was during this time that my brother Tony made the poor choice of not following one of the rules set forth by the school administrators—or was it the Archdiocese, or the Pope—I'm not sure. The offense? Talking in the lunch line, a modern-day sin for Catholic-school kids. Talking in a lunch line was an obvious detriment to society, to religiosity, possibly to humanity itself, not to mention it really hosed up efficient food pick-up. Plus, if talking in a lunch line became permissible, what next? Kids would think they were free to chew on a pencil during a math test, or whistle while they walked down the halls. Some things had to be stopped.

From across the cafeteria, Clodhopper's beady eyes scanned the room left-to-right, on the lookout for miscreants. Do-badders. Kids who liked to chat socially while they waited in a line because there was absolutely nothing else to do. She fixed on the eighth-grade boys near tray pick-up, and bristled.

Who's talking? That Bob-zeen boy?
Blasphemous heathen!
Cloven-hooved infidel!
Rotten fu**ing kid!

Sister's rheumy eyes blazed. In a righteous huff, she waddled toward the line of boys, hefting her heavy black dress with both hands while her enormous bosom swung back and forth like a giant double-barreled pendulum. She, and it, came to rest just shy of my brother, where she started screaming her fat face off.

"There's no talking in the lunch line!" she hissed at Tony, then grabbed his cheek and shook it violently. "Just because your *mother* is in the hospital having a *hysterectomy* doesn't mean you can get away with *talking in the lunch line!*"

She shook some more, and Tony had no choice but to stand there and take it while the whole school watched. She finally let go, and even from a few tables away, I could see the blood red circle on Tony's cheek.

Lord help me, at that moment, I hated Sister Clotildis with every ounce of my fifty-pound being—my entire heart and soul was full of it. Hate, that is. I wanted to run over and stab her with my little plastic cafeteria knife, but I knew if I did that, my parents would definitely be called. And Mom was in the hospital; she didn't need the aggravation.

I guess it's possible Tony *was* acting up, bragging about Mom's hysterectomy; showing off to his eighth-grade buddies. *Heh—your mom has endometriosis? Dude, have her go and get her whole uterus removed, then come talk to me!*

Tony was taught a valuable lesson that day, one that

ostensibly stayed with him into adulthood, and the lesson was: *Don't talk in lunch lines.* At least not when there's an obese, child-hating nun around.

And if you thought you were safe after making it out of the lunch line with your face and/or dignity intact, well, think again. Sister Clotildis had two main jobs in the cafeteria. Priority 1 was ensuring no child made sound while in the line; and P2: guarding the garbage cans.

Sister Clotildis stood sentry at the three cafeteria garbage bins each and every day at the lunch hour, watching for non-finishers, because at Sorrows, if you ate hot lunch, you were not allowed to throw any leftovers away. Your parents paid for it, it was your stomach and your body and your hypothalamus, but you were not allowed to make the decision as to when you wanted to stop eating. This was a rule. In order to throw any food away, you had to get past Sister Clotildis at the garbage station, which was not easy—literally or figuratively.

If Clodhopper caught you at the garbage cans with food on your tray, she sent you back to your table to finish it. As a kid who hated all vegetables, this was extremely anxiety-producing for me. I'd heard stories of kids trying to sneak their unwanted food into the trash—stuffing disgusting cafeteria vegetables into their milk cartons in an attempt to get the contraband past Clotildis.

Legend was that if Clodhopper caught you trying to throw your nasty scraps out in your milk carton, she waddled you back to your table and spoke gravely about the starving children in Africa or India or Troutdale or wherever until you finished your foul, milky peas.

I brought cold lunch every day.

* * *

Sister Clotildis could be mellow at times. Like when she read to us in class and fell asleep.

During a.m. story time, Clodhopper sat at her desk at the front of the room while we listened to her read unenthusiastically about the antics of Dick and Jane and their dog Spot. It was a regular occurrence for Sister to start nodding off while reading aloud. I can't blame her. The Dick and Jane stories were *pretty* dry, and with the sun streaming through the huge classroom windows, the room was nice and toasty, just like old people liked it.

In the middle of a Dick and Jane story, things would get quiet. The reading would stop for a few long seconds, and Sister's breathing would become slow and regular. In a minute, she'd be out. We'd all look at each other and shrug—*Our parents are paying for this?*—and by Thanksgiving break, my classmates and I had seen it fifty times. We'd sit idly, drumming our fingers on our desks, doodling on a notepad, restless, yet grateful for this tender mercy: while Clotildis dozed, we were safe. We couldn't get in trouble for touching our hair or licking our lips; glancing out the window to look at a bird.

When we realized Sister was entering the REM stage, we'd look around the room, each of us with the same thought: *Now? Should we wake her up now? What if she sleeps through lunch?!* Finally, someone in class would take it upon himself to fake a cough to jolt her awake. The boys took turns. Marcus or Tommy or Angelo would cough, and Sister would jerk awake, smack her gums together like an ancient obese tortoise, and get right back to the story as if she hadn't just been sleeping.

I'm sure she was tired, exhausted, probably. She really should have retired years ago. Or at least died.

* * *

We had a sweet girl in our class who sometimes arrived late in the morning. Her name was Tonya, and Sister liked to call Tonya out whenever she was tardy. Arriving late at Our Lady of Sorrows was perhaps not as serious an offense as talking in a line, but was of course frowned upon, and a display of disrespect to the classroom. A punishable offense, for sure, one that warranted at least some level of shaming.

"Tonya likes to have attention walking in late to class," Sister would say to the rest of us as Tonya rushed in a few minutes late. "We'll give her the attention she wants."

Sister would call Tonya to stand at the front of the room so we could all stare. Tonya, the tiniest girl in class, even smaller than me, would walk meekly to the front, her chin quivering already. I felt sorry for Tonya. She was a nice person, and had given me a Three Musketeers bar the day after Halloween. She was my friend. And who knew why she was late? Maybe Tonya's mom was a drinker and Tonya had to walk to school that day because her mom didn't get out of bed. Or maybe her mom took care of the sick grandma and ran late on occasion. Or maybe her mom was a single parent with a crappy car and she had to get a jump that morning. Clodhopper didn't ask for a reason, though; she just told Tonya to come to the front and stand. We were all forced to look at her for the next five minutes as she held her hands behind her back, stared at her shoes, and cried huge tears that fell onto the floor.

* * *

Another boy came late in the year. His name was John, and John had an odd way about him; a nervous habit of some kind. It was as if he was unable to control the sounds and movements that he made.

From his first day in class, John twitched and grunted. At first I thought he was just clearing his throat or twitching away a bothersome gnat; then I noticed he did it all the time, and it wasn't a grunt here or a grunt there or a twitch every now and again. It was *errrnnnt, errrnnnt, errrnnnt, twitch, twitch, twitch,* all day long.

John would grunt—*Errrrrrnt*—then scrunch up his face in a conspicuous pucker, and complete the sequence with a hard blink of his eyes. He went through a whole *grunt-scrunch-blink* cycle, all day.

"Errrrrnnnt!" *Scrunch, blink.*

"Errrrrnnnt!" *Scrunch, blink.*

The scrunching and the blinking, at times, came before the grunting, but regardless, it was a whole deal, a complete tic rotation, a trifecta of peculiarity. Ongoing. *Grunt, scrunch, blink. Scrunch, blink, grunt.* During math with Clodhopper, music with Mrs. Kregel, in the middle of the Pledge of Allegiance, the morning "Our Father," in the lunch line—John grunted and blinked. I wondered why he didn't just stop it! Nobody in their right mind would do this, especially if they were the new kid in class and learning hour-by-hour that their teacher was an 80-year-old child-hating nun with a charcoal briquette for a heart.

By the third straight day of his incessant twitching and grunting, when Sister realized that this was no anomaly or occasional wiggle, she brought John to the front of the class and announced her plan to cure him of his affliction: humiliation. Humiliation must have been a class they taught at nun school, right along with Biblical Theology and Phonics for Elementary Age.

Clotildis placed John near her desk so, like tardy Tonya, she could sit a few feet away and soberly discuss his shortcomings while the class stared.

But a simple stare-down wasn't enough for Sister Clotildis, not for John's type of misbehavior. No, your run-of-the-mill, off-the-shelf cruelty would not do.

John stood and faced his classmates.

"People!" Sister squawked. (She always called us *people*. I hated her.) "John seems to want a lot of attention. When he does his noises and movements, I want you to do those things back at him. Maybe then he'll stop."

Ummmm, what?

We were all supposed to grunt now? And scrunch up our faces? Was this an order? I considered myself an obedient child, but this seemed extreme. And weird. I looked around at my classmates and saw similar looks of confusion and discomfort. I certainly didn't feel like grunting and scrunching up my face in front of everyone, and anyway, I didn't care if the kid grunted! It took the focus off me and my punishable nail-biting.

John remained at the front of the silent classroom, turning purple and trying his best to become part of the floor. He twitched slightly, and blinked like he was trudging through a sandstorm, but he held it together. No grunting.

Sister Clotildis stopped talking, let the quiet settle in, and turned to John. She nodded gravely, as if she was just this moment becoming certain that this form of "discipline" was for the good; that she was teaching John a valuable life lesson. *Someday, he'd thank her for this.*

The class stared in silence at the new kid, the kid with the problem. Even *I* found it agonizing, and I wasn't the one standing at the front of the room like some petty criminal in the town square stocks. I looked down at my desktop and fiddled with my pencils. Sister finally excused him to his seat. The order stood, however: *Today, we mock John.*

I looked over at him, in the row to my left, seated now in his all-in-one desk and chair. He was a big kid, too big for these desks, and he sat stuffed in his seat, twitching and moving; his bungee-cord arms wrapped around his torso as if he were spring-loaded. He gripped his body with all his might, his face contorting slightly and his head jerking here and there, but he did not grunt. It must have taken every ounce of will and strength to sit there while twenty-three sets of eyes bore down.

I turned away from John and put my attention to the true irritant sitting in the row to my right: Marcus Navin-Johnson, who was busy making noises and spazzing out as well, and not due to any diagnosable neurological disorder. A cross between Dudley Do-Right, William F. Buckley, Jr., and Harpo Marx, Marcus was simply and inherently annoying. Loud. Rude. Excellent at math. He really *did* want all the attention. And Sister loved him.

I'd known Marcus since the first grade, and could tell what was going on in that bloated brain of his. He had his eyes on John. This directive Sister had just issued caused him to become visibly excited. To be granted permission to act out in class, to make an obnoxious and irritating noise, to mock someone, with holy sanction? Marcus was jacked—actually bouncing up and down in his seat, eyeballing his target. Ever-obedient Marcus. He couldn't wait to get his grunt on.

Not long after word came down from on fat that we were to let John have it with some mock grunting and blinking, poor John started in with his routine. Slowly at first. A warm-up after his few minutes of self-imposed quiet.

"Errnnt." *Blink.*

"Errnnnnt." *Scrunch.*

Then it came—a great grunting attack indeed; he'd held on so long. He sat at his desk and fell into a massive grunting, twitching, blinking seizure.

"ERRRNNNT!" *Blink. Scrunch.*

"ERRRNNNT!" *Blink. Scrunch.*

Maybe it *was* a good thing he was so crammed into his seat; otherwise, he might have fallen out of it.

Following instructions, Marcus geared up. From his desk two rows over, William F. Buckley-Moron—Marcus—turned his entire body toward John, and bellowed out for all to hear, "John! John! John! ERRRNNNNNNTT!"

BLINK!

John turned to Marcus, lowered his eyes, and slumped further in his little chair. He let out a small, "Errrrnt," followed by a tiny blink and a nearly imperceptible scrunch.

The poor kid. I don't know how he made it through the year.

Chapter Eighteen

And if Catholic school wasn't bad enough, what with the hard math and the resident wrecker of childhoods, we had to go to Mass a minimum of twice a week. More punishment!

Attending Mass on Sundays was a given, pretty much a requirement for Catholics, and attending at least one extra day per week was an unwritten rule for the students at Sorrows. Maybe it wasn't unwritten at all; it might have been part of the contract—they needed to fill the seats. Our family followed the rules and regs: we kids went to Mass on Sundays with Mom and Dad and did the extra weekday service at the school church, too.

Our bonus day of Mass was Wednesday, which offered a little buffer on either side of the real holy day; time to recover from the previous Sunday's monotony and boredom, and to mentally prepare for and dread the next. On Wednesdays, Mom drove us to school early, pulled the car up to the curb in front, and my siblings and I tumbled out, traipsing across the blacktop parking lot (which was also the playground) and into the chapel.

Sunday Mass was unpleasant, don't get me wrong, but weekday Mass seemed another thing altogether: rushed and more meaningless, if that was possible. As if everyone there, Father Pasqual included, knew we were on a time crunch and had to move it along. The kids had to get to class, and Father—well, rumor was that Wednesday was the morning he met with his wine rep. He had to *get*. The strongest desire of all weekday Mass-goers seemed to be this: *Let it be over.*

If you're familiar with Catholic Mass, you know it's boring. If you're not familiar, let me tell you. It's boring. And repetitious. Time after time, week after week, it's the same thing. Every day is a rerun. The first half hour consists of a bunch of standing up, sitting down, and repeating nonsense words. After that, it's more kneeling, standing, sitting, a few depressing hymns thrown in, then more repetitive prayers and phrases recited back to the priest. I'd be exhausted after every service—from all the first-half calisthenics for one thing, and the effort of simply trying to stay awake for the rest. Each time, I'd walk out of the sanctuary bleary-eyed and stiff. It was like walking out of the coal mines into the light of day, sometimes even down to the ashes on my face.

And poor Father Pasqual, what a job he had. A new sermon for each Mass? Plus the extra one on Saturday evening for the people who had plans to be hungover on Sunday morning? That's the equivalent of writing a fifteen hundred word newspaper column every day, on deadline!

Brutal. Catholic priests were the Mike Roykos of the theological world. And no Internet to copy from.

For each service, we listened to Father's sermons: his speeches discussing the role of Judas at the Last Supper; the symbolism of Jonah surviving the belly of the whale; the underlying theme of the Ten Plagues; Lent.

Lent! Lent was crazy talk. Forty days and nights of going without something I loved, in the name of religion? Every year, I tried to make sense of Lent, the extended Catholic anti-holiday. Give up candy? Or my favorite TV show? Was there a point? How was Lent any different than any month at our house? My whole year was Lent.

"Spiritual self-discipline," Father Pasqual said. "A fast for the soul," he said. Me missing *I Dream of Jeannie* for a month or giving up the few antique Brach candies I might have gotten at my grandma's once a week was going to fortify my soul? I got plenty of real-life discipline at home from Dad, and Mom never bought us candy, so I was all set, thanks, God.

Lent, to me, was not relatable. Sermons, repetitions, the kissing of chalices, not relatable. And don't get me started on the Ten Plagues. God couldn't have been that mean.

There was *one* good thing about church, though: Communion. I liked eating, and the beautiful, pristine communion wafers were yummy—and extra special since it was the only time I ever got white bread. Thin as a piece of card stock, the wafers crackled and crunched in my mouth like a perfect little bready potato chip. *Tasty.* Every Mass, I fantasized about grabbing the whole bowl, heading back to my seat in the pew and munching on the delicious church chips at my leisure, like popcorn at a movie. A really boring one. Eating a bowlful of communions would have killed about ten minutes.

I guess we were lucky. Some parents made their kids go to church more than one day per school week, like Tuesdays *and* Thursdays, or Mondays, Wednesdays *and* Fridays. I felt for those kids. They had it worse than we did. How could any parent or nun or priest think that making a kid go to Mass several times a week was going to do any good? Didn't they hear our complaining? Did they not see our dead eyes as we walked out of church?

I've yet to meet a Catholic who's said, "I loved going to church three or four times a week when I was a child. It made me the good person I am, and I'm glad of it." I've heard mostly the opposite from the recovering Catholics I've known: "Going to Mass three or four times a week made me the person I am today—which is an atheist."

* * *

Church was boring and monotonous, and I might have hated it, but that would have been a sin.

Sister Clotildis taught us that we weren't allowed to "hate" anything. God created everything, so if you "hated" anything, you hated God. You couldn't even hate the Devil!

Marcus Navin-Johnson, our class's annoying over-achiever and Clodhopper's pet, made it his life's mission to holler out, "You hate God!" if ever I breathed the word *hate* in class or the lunchroom or on the playground, no matter the object of my hatred.

"I hate this pencil," I would say as I sat at my desk with my crummy No. 3 pencil.

"*You hate God!*" Marcus would stage-whisper from his

desk, without looking up.

"I hate long division," I'd say during math.

"*You hate God!*" he'd say, as he whipped through his worksheet.

"I hate creamed corn," I would say in the lunchroom.

"*You hate God!*" Marcus would holler from two seats down, his mouth full of food.

"No I don't! I just hate creamed corn! And long division! And number three pencils!"

And you, Marcus Navin-Johnson.

Hating confession had to have been a sin, too, but I couldn't help myself.

Confession: your invitation to step into a darkened closet, kneel on a block of wood and whisper your "sins" to the parish priest, the guy who sat comfortably on the other side of an oversized, mesh-covered peephole. Confession made as much sense to me as having ashes shmushed on your forehead by a man in a robe.

During Catechism, Sister Clotildis taught us the reason we had to go to confession: original sin.

"All humans have sin, they're born with it," she explained. It was all on account of Adam and Eve; something to do with the Garden of Eden? And apples and snakes? Or was it apples and oranges? I can't remember all the details, but the gist of it was that we had to confess the things we'd done wrong, receive our penance of twenty "Our Fathers" and forty "Hail Marys" from Father Pasqual so we could be cleansed of our sins and still attend Mass on Sundays and also get the hot chocolate and donuts afterward in the gym.

Kneeling in a creepy, cramped closet that smelled like feet and whispering secrets to a grown man was weird enough, but the worst part was, I had to lie. In confession! The holy phone booth. Every single time.

It's not like I was out spray-painting the sides of buildings and breaking into cars in my spare time. *I was nine.* I was barely allowed to chew gum. My parents were super strict, and we got away with nothing. Our TV watching was restricted. *Laugh-In* was off limits—too racy. Same with *Love, American Style*—too much kissing. We weren't allowed to swear. *Butt* and *fart* were bad words in our house; Dad required that we use *rump* and *pass gas.* The word *panties?* Never uttered in our home. Mom called them bloomers.

And we were by no means ever allowed to take the Lord's name in vain, at home or at school. We couldn't say "God" in anger, amazement, or indignation. *Gosh* or *golly* were almost too close. At school, we could get away with using *guy* as an interjection. (*"Guy, we have so much homework!"* or, *"Guy, Marcus Navin-Johnson is such an idiot!"*) Dad took the Lord's name in vain like crazy, and I heard other swear words from him, but they were strictly forbidden to us kids. We had *guy.*

So I didn't swear, I didn't lie, I didn't steal, I didn't disobey my parents, and I didn't take the Lord's name in vain. I was an innocent child! I hardly did anything wrong—I was way too scared of my parents and teachers to do anything wrong. But every two weeks we were forced to go to confession and confess something, so I had to make stuff up.

Of course, just like Mass, confession was a requirement for Catholic children because they're inherently rotten, lying, sinning little bastards. I knew this, for the Bible told me so. I was not a liar, but there was not a single instance during my years at Catholic school when I did *not* lie in confession.

It was practically the only time I did.

On confession day, we formed two single-file lines and followed Sister Clotildis up the main hall and into the chapel for our appointments. We all knew the drill, but as we waited in the vestibule for our turn in the Catholic penalty box, Sister gave us tips and suggestions as to what we might confess—talking points, if you will—in case any of us needed reminders of how we were bad. Possible sins included stealing, disobeying, back-talking, not finishing your dinner, wasting milk on your morning cereal, lisping, being pigeon-toed or left-handed, having bad thoughts. *Having bad thoughts made the list!?* I was in trouble.

We entered the dim, quiet church, the pews aglow with muted stained-glass color beams, the smell of candle wax and Pledge furniture polish floating on the air, and made our way to the confessionals at the side of the sanctuary. I fell into line alongside my classmates and geared up, preparing my lies, trying to put my list into some logical order. I was like a criminal wracking his brain, scrambling to invent a plausible story before going into the interrogation room. But I didn't have anything believable! Life at home was orderly and structured. My worst offense this week had been swishing my potatoes around on my plate in an effort to fool Mom into thinking I'd taken my one required bite. But not eating your potatoes wasn't a sin, was it?

Marcus Navin-Johnson walked into the confessional.

I took a step forward in line.

I needed to come up with something quick—it was almost my turn! I needed to put a new twist on an old sin!

Did I use "disobeyed my mother" last time? What's another word for disobey? Think! Think!

My turn came. Marcus walked out of the booth, smiling. "Have fun in there, Bob-*zeen*," he said in his annoying voice. At least he pronounced my name right. I wondered what he'd confessed—that he was the most irritating person on the planet? I stepped into the sock closet, which unfortunately now smelled less like socks and more like Marcus. I waved my hand around in front of my face to clear the air, and made a mental note to remind Marcus that next confession day, he might think about getting his farts out before he stepped into God's holy nook.

I kneeled on the miniature bench, triggering the red light outside of the confessional, a signal to the waiting sinners (and non-sinning liars) that this booth was taken.

Ocupado.

~~*Interrogation*~~ *Confession in Progress.*

I folded my hands and put my face closer to the mesh window. I recognized Father Pasqual on the other side—you could totally see through it.

I took a breath, and opened the session with my only true statement: "Bless me, Father, for I have sinned. It's been two weeks since my last confession.

"I disobeyed my mother. (*Lie.*)

"I disobeyed my father. (*Lie.*)

"I took the Lord's name in vain. (*Lie.*)

"I said a swear word. (*Lie.*)

"I stole a piece of candy from the store. (*Lie.*)

"I thought bad thoughts about Sister Clotildis. (*Not a lie.*)

"I hate Catholic school."

"*You hate God!*"

"GUY!!!"

Chapter Nineteen

Terri sat in our big green chair in the living room, drinking tea and studying, and Mitzi worked with Andy on his spelling at the dining room table. Mom had finished in the kitchen, and sat on the couch with our huge wicker laundry basket at her feet, folding clothes. Annie helped her with towels. I leaned against the couch beside Mom and did my homework, practicing my cursive. A typical fall school night.

A stream of cold air followed Dad in as he opened the front door. He'd been outside, getting something from the car. He shook off the rain and hung his coat on the rack in the foyer.

After my homework, I moved on to "Beauty Pageant," a game I'd made up where I drew the faces of four girls with different hair styles and face shapes and put them in adjacent boxes, like *Hollywood Squares*. After drawing all four faces, I gave them names like Dena, Kitty, Carol Ann and Tiffany, and picked the girl I thought was the prettiest, adding stars all around her head.

The phone rang. "I'll get it!" I said, and hopped up from the floor. Even though Dad was a freak about manners and required that we answer the phone in a certain manner, which was, "Bobzien residence, (state your name) speaking," I still liked to be the one to answer. I'd given up caring if I sounded like a dork; I wanted to know who was on the phone.

It was Sister Alphonsine, the principal of our school, asking to speak to my father.

What's she calling for? I wondered. The school hardly ever called; the only time was maybe when the PTA needed to talk to Mom about the annual Spaghetti Dinner. "Hold on, please," I said to Sister.

I walked into the kitchen, and from the top of the stairs called down for Dad, who had gone to the basement to tinker at his workbench. He came up, wiping his hands on a garage towel, and I returned to my beauty pageant and my spot in front of the couch.

Dad took the phone at the small desk in the dining room and began the conversation with Sister Alphonsine using the usual niceties—*Yes, hello, oh, fine. How are you, Sister.*

He didn't say much for the next few minutes, just a couple *mmm-hmms* and *is-that-rights*? Sister seemed to be doing most of the talking, and something was wrong, I could tell by Dad's manner and tone. And forehead. The veins were starting to bulge.

The call from school had to do with Tony.

Tony, my cool brother, who could do anything: run fast, play baseball, build stuff, and do that whistling thing with his hands cupped over his mouth. Tony, the kid who replaced the handlebars of his bike with a steering wheel from a real car. Tony, who covered nearly a square mile on Halloween night and came home with a pillowcase absolutely stuffed with candy.

Tony, the known prankster.

Dad finished the conversation with our principal with a terse, "Yes, thank you, Sister. Of course. Goodnight now," and hung up the phone, softly and slowly, conscious of stopping himself from slamming it into the cradle and breaking it into parts. He stared down at the phone for a couple seconds, took a deep breath—a sign of bad things to come—and turned to Mom.

He relayed the story for all of us to hear. About Tony and Rhonda Richards.

I knew Rhonda from school. She was one of the prettiest girls at Sorrows. When you're in the lower grades at a K-through-8 school, you notice the popular eighth-grade girls. I saw Rhonda in the halls and cafeteria and admired her long, shiny brown hair and the way it swung side-to-side when she walked, just like Jan Brady's. I'd heard Tony talk about her recently. I think he liked her. Or maybe he didn't at all. I couldn't tell.

Dad told Mom that Rhonda's mother had called the school today to speak with Sister Alphonsine. Seemed someone had let the air out of Rhonda's bicycle tires and she'd had to walk her bike home in the rain. She'd been carrying an instrument of some kind with her, too, one that may have been ruined on account of the downpour. Tony had done it. It was corroborated, confirmed somehow. No presumed innocence until proven guilty here; this was Catholic school. The nuns knew everything.

Dad looked around the living room, scanning for Tony, an expression on his face a combination of frustration, exhaustion, and anger. Mostly anger. Dad took extreme pride in his children's good behavior, and now our school's principal had to call him at home to inform him that one of his children, his number one son, had done something so awful, so ungentlemanly, that a girl had to walk her bike home in the rain, two or three miles it was, *and* it got her flute case all wet?

Tony was dead meat.

"Where is he?" Dad asked Mom, and took another deep breath.

Dad called for Tony, and those of us in the room tensed. We all knew what was coming down the pike after this phone call: a lecture from Dad, and it was going to be a whopper. The lecture Dad was about to deliver over this antic was not the type we got for playing volleyball in the house and knocking over a lamp. This lecture wasn't going to be the one we got for putting an empty carton of milk back in the fridge. This lecture was going to go down in history. We were about to witness the lecture of the year. Maybe the decade! Sister Alphonsine had to call our dad!

Get underground!

Tony walked into the dining room and the atmosphere changed; the barometric pressure actually rose, or dropped, whichever it is when somebody's ass was fixing to become grass. Tony stood in front of Dad, who started in with the stern looks, the dramatic breathing and barrage of questions, some answerable, some not.

"Is this true, Tony?" he asked. "Did you let the air out of this girl's tires?"

Answerable. Tony nodded slightly.

"Yes or no, son," Dad said.

"Yes," he said, looking at the floor.

"Would you like to look at me when I talk to you?"

Tony raised his eyes to the general vicinity of our father's face, and with his peripheral vision was most likely able to see the frown, possibly the bulging veins in Dad's bald head, but no answer came.

"Would you like to tell me why you did this?" Dad asked.

Unanswerable, obviously. Tony could have said, *I was making a memory with my friends? Girls get together and French-braid each other's hair, and boys pull pranks on the girls we like? Or don't like?* No, that would not have done: Tony remained silent.

"I think you know better, son. Don't you know better than this?" Tony knew better, and nodded. He was wilting.

"You know, I'm very disappointed in you, Tony," Dad said. "Extremely disappointed."

The disappointment. Dad didn't need to spank or slap or beat us. Nothing was worse than disappointing Dad. My stomach was starting to knot.

I went back to my sketch pad, and Dad let the silence sink in. No one spoke or moved. I stopped my drawing and glanced again at Tony, red-faced and blotchy. I turned toward Annie, sitting with her knees to her chest near the laundry basket, and we caught eyes. Her chin was quivering, and she looked away. Andy sat at the dining room table, staring blankly at his homework, and Mitzi picked at her nails. I started to not feel good. I don't think I'd ever seen Dad this mad.

Tony stood in front of Dad, on the verge of tears, trying to keep it together until the punishment was declared complete and he was formally excused. He'd be sent to bed after this; it was almost time anyway, and at this point, being sent to bed would be welcome.

"Do you think you've learned your lesson?" Dad said. At last, a concluding question, an answerable one, and Tony said yes. His shoulders relaxed. A few long, silent seconds went by, and we were done. And when I say we, I mean we. When Dad gave a lecture, it was for everyone's benefit. You can be assured no kid in this family was ever going to let the air out of anyone's tires, not as long as they lived. Not even if they were asked to. If any of my siblings had aspirations of becoming a bicycle mechanic, well, that dream was squashed as of today.

But wait.

Dad stepped over to the desk and pulled out the White Pages. He flopped the thick phone book onto our small, antique roll-top and opened it up to the *R*'s.

"Son, you're going to call Rhonda and apologize to her," he said. "And to her mother."

Did I say dead meat earlier? This was beyond dead meat. This was trampled, squished, maggoty, rotting, forgotten-in-a-camping-cooler-for-the-summer dead meat. Regular dead meat sounded pretty good all of a sudden. Appetizing even. Poor Tony.

Dad dialed the number. "You ask for Mrs. Richards first," he said, and handed the phone to my brother.

I saw Tony's face contort and his eyes well up, and that feeling came on for real: the one I got when I was sad and couldn't swallow. My throat hurt. I didn't think the prank was that big of a deal. I'd taken much worse from Tony and sometimes never even told. And maybe Rhonda Richards deserved it. Maybe she did something to Tony first! Geez, I didn't know! I just knew I hated to see my brother get in so much trouble. Tony was mean sometimes, but he never really hurt me that bad, and he did play catch with me and stuff. He was a good brother. I didn't understand why Dad had to get so mad about everything.

After a few rings, someone at the Richards' answered, probably in a normal way, like with the word "Hello."

I scooted from my spot in front of the couch to the heat vent in the corner and pushed myself against the wall. I watched as Tony, crimson now, apologized, choking out the words, "I'm sorry," ("Sorry for what," Dad said) to Mrs. Richards and then her daughter.

I tried not to let Tony see that I was watching. I looked down at my beauty pageant drawings and scribbled out all of the faces. I looked back at Tony, crying on the phone. I felt like crying myself.

Chapter Twenty

"Entry forms for Rose Festival Princess tryouts are on the bookcase by the door," Sister Clotildis said. "Girls may pick one up on the way out. Single file!" I had tuned Clodhopper out as she'd droned on during the last few minutes of class with the usual end-of-day reminders—*Chairs on desks, people! Latin stems homework due tomorrow!*—but my ears perked up at the mention of a competition. *Princess tryouts?* That sounded doable. I grabbed an entry form off the top of the bookcase and headed out.

I knew a little about the Rose Festival, Portland's annual summertime jubilee, with its parades, dragon boat races, visiting Naval ships and waterfront carnival. I knew that as part of the festival, one twelfth-grade girl from each of the city's ten high schools was chosen to represent her school as a princess on the Senior Court, and in recent years, a Junior Court—eight elementary school girls chosen as princesses—had been added to the festivities. These princesses, big and small, represented the city in various Festival activities: presiding over events and parades, greeting visiting dignitaries from sister cities, singing songs at old folks' homes, and word on the street was they got a bunch of free clothes.

I ran into the house after school and went straight to the kitchen to show Mom the entry form for the tryout. I held it in front of her face while she peeled potatoes at the sink.

"Princess tryouts?" she said, pulling her face away from the paper I'd put two inches from her eyes. "What?" She went right on peeling, my opposite-of-stage mother. Mom was not only uninterested, she actually discouraged this kind of thing—pageants and plays and theatrics—plus she was *way* too busy: feeding seven kids each and every night, canning the tomatoes, and contemplating a divorce from Dad.

She finished up with the potatoes, dried her hands on a dish towel and took the form from me.

"Oh, gosh," she frowned. "You sure you want to do this? It sounds time-consuming."

What was wrong with my mother? Always worried about time. Was I sure? Of course I was sure! I had a chance to be *a princess*. Go places. Get new clothes. Eat restaurant food. And all for free! What could she possibly object to? Things were weird and depressing at home; having a princess in the house would cheer everybody up! I didn't wait for permission. I was doing this.

The entry form had all the details: logistical info, suggestions for attire, and a statement recommending that participants have a speech, poem, or other oratory piece prepared in the event they made it to the final round of the competition.

The next day, I got to work preparing. I found a book of poems in the library at school and decided on a catchy piece that would be my speech for the finals. "Pachycephalosaurus", a poem by Richard Armour about a hard-headed dinosaur, had a pleasing ABAB rhyme scheme. Short enough to memorize, long enough to make an impression. I also began the task of developing my curtsy, which, I learned, was a major part of the whole princess deal—an official job requirement! My curtsy consisted of a grand sweeping motion of my scrawny arm in front of my scrawny body, a graceful drop to one knee—I was used to this from genuflecting at church—and an understated finish: a bow of the head and a flip of the wrist. Elegant and effortless, with a touch of whimsy, was what I was going for.

Speech practice and curtsy modifications became nightly activities for the next four weeks. Mitzi, Terri and Annie critiqued my curtsy and listened to me recite my poem night after night until, finally, I was lucky if I could get even one of them to give me the time of day. As the competition neared, I could coerce Annie into being my audience of one, but she was over giving critiques or feedback. Actually, she barely pretended to pay attention. I would seek her out in the TV room, turn the volume down and start in on my Packy poem. She'd sprawl on the couch, look up at the ceiling and reflexively move her lips in unison with mine as I recited my speech. For the hundredth time.

The night of the tryout finally came, and I was as ready as I'd ever be. My speech was down. My curtsy I could have done in my sleep, and I probably did. I got dressed on try-out night in the one and only dress I owned: a long, purple Bohemian-style maxi with a lace bib front. Even though I was a tomboy and hated dresses, I knew what was expected of a potential princess, and I wanted to win. I wanted those new clothes!

Terri and Annie helped with my coiffure that evening, working my hair into the popular style of the day: the do made famous by fashion icon Jan Brady. This hairstyle was achieved by taking a small section of hair on either side of my middle part and clipping it back loosely with a barrette. What you got with "The Jan" was a hairdo resembling a set of living room drapes, secured with tiebacks. These were the days before the use of extensions and hair gel; before loco pageant moms were decking their six-year-olds out in acrylic nails and Spanx. It was a small miracle we scrounged up two semi-matching barrettes.

My front teeth were the next issue. One large square Chiclet of a permanent tooth had come in in front, and beside it, a tiny baby tooth dangled. Asymmetry may have been a desirable look when it came to art or fashion, but not so much with teeth. In addition to my imbalanced choppers, a weird growth had developed on my gum line, directly above my loose baby tooth. This growth was a perfect circle, and filled with something. Pus, probably. A "gum pimple" is what it was. Noticeable for sure, but only if I smiled. It might have been an abscess, but was never officially diagnosed. Mom was too preoccupied with other pressing matters to take me to the dentist for something as inconsequential as an abscess! It would heal itself in due time.

Front and center, what you saw when I smiled were a

bunch of odd-sized, mismatched teeth and a noticeable gum wart. Didn't stop me from smiling, though. I was going to princess tryouts! I had a meaty poem to worry about. Curtsies to execute. Preparedness was all that was on my mind. Not disproportionate teeth or abscessed gums.

A buzz filled the house as we prepared to leave for tryouts. Annie and Terri were going to come along, and Aunt Billie was over that night, so she was on board. And even though my mom wasn't pushing me to do it, or enthusiastic about it, or really very interested in taking me, I think deep down she was OK with it. She was at least dropping me off, I knew that.

The nerves were starting to hit. I practiced my poem as I paced the living room floor and hyperventilated, waiting for Mom to get done with the dinner dishes. *"Among the later dinosaurs, though not the largest, strongest*—let's go!— *Pachysephalosaurus had the name that was the longest.* Mom!"

She rushed out of the kitchen and grabbed her purse and a paperback.

As I headed for the front door, Tony stopped me in the living room for a little pep talk; a talk only a big brother could give. He laid on the couch, inspecting a tennis ball he'd cut in half with an Xacto knife. He stuck his leg out, turning himself into a human turnstile.

"You're not going to win, you know," he said.

Blink. Blink. Blink.

I looked at Tony, and as my eyes landed upon his delicate cheekbones and big brown eyes, I wondered how that pretty mouth could say those dirty words.

"You're not gonna win, so don't get your hopes up," he repeated, studying the innards of the ball, and also making a point of not looking my way.

I was stunned into silence. Had I just been bitch slapped? I may as well have been. *Not going to win?* What did that mean? Not winning had simply not occurred to me. Winning was the only thing that *had* occurred to me—the only thing I had visualized since picking up that form in Sister Clotildis's class. The practicing and preparing—the poem, the curtsy, the smile, the acceptance speech—all this work was in preparation for winning. Winning!

"Well, *somebody*'s got to win," I said.

"Well, it's not going to be you."

"*Well somebody's got to win!*"

Wicked comeback. I pushed his leg away, ran out of the house and got in the car with my sisters, aunt and mom. Tony didn't come. I didn't *want* Tony to come. He wasn't invited. Tony and his negative mojo could just stay the heck away from princess tryouts!

The contest was held at Cleveland High, a few miles from home. We walked into the auditorium, packed with people and humming with the sound of 300 excited, murmuring voices.

Mom and I made our way to the organizers and I was instructed to go backstage along with a hundred or more girls, many decked out in beautiful dresses and shiny headbands, each one smiling and anxious, hoping to wow the judges and leave the auditorium as a real, live princess.

The organizers gathered all the girls into haphazard lines, and I was handed a paper plate with the number 67 written in felt pen. The plate was one of those thin, flimsy jobs that couldn't have been intended to hold any real food, but to me it was special: my Golden Ticket; a chintzy one, sure, but it would have to do the trick as an identifying system at princess tryouts, plus it gave us contestants something to hold on to.

Backstage, the organizers told us how the contest was to go. Several rounds would take place throughout the evening. For each round, ten girls would walk on stage, face the audience and the judges, and answer the question posed to them by the emcee. Based on poise, clarity, and the quality of the responses, the judges would select one, two, or three girls from each batch of ten, and these lucky and talented girls would move on to the next round. Every round's questions would increase in difficulty, and the last round would showcase the eight finalists, who would deliver their prepared speeches.

Losers got to keep their paper plates.

The contest commenced.

I sat in the contestants' section of the auditorium and checked out the lower numbers, the tens and twenties and thirties—my competition—as they walked up the side steps and onto the stage. From here I was able to focus on the pretty dresses, the white tights and the clean, shiny shoes. I winced at the sight of a few contestants who possessed the thing every girl my age wanted. Coveted.

Ringlets!

Blast!

I touched my barrettes. Still there.

I ran my tongue over my gum wart. Also still there.

The first round question was simple. It came from the woman emceeing the show, a lovely lady with fluffy, upswept silver hair and lots of creamy blush. Her voice was a lilting melody—a bouquet of flowers—and she spoke sweetly, clearly, and slowly into her small, silver microphone, which she held for each contestant: "Please tell us your name, your age, and the name of the school you attend."

Well, if you couldn't answer this "question" with any confidence, more than likely you didn't have your curtsy locked down or a killer ABAB rhyming poem committed to memory, I was pretty sure of that. I watched from the sidelines as several of the girls seemed to be temporarily paralyzed by this most basic of questions. The audience, the lights, the pressure—it was a lot—but still, come on! *Pull yourselves together!* I couldn't wait to get on stage.

The forties and fifties got their shot, and finally, I was called up with the rest of the sixties, and the lady repeated the question for our group. When my turn came, I did what I'd come to do: I answered. I spoke it loud and proud. I knew my damn name!

I made it through, while the judges weeded out the mentally inert. On to Round Two!

The field had been cut by less than half; and again, in groups of ten, the contestants walked on stage for the next round's question.

"If you could have any type of pet, what would it be, and why?" asked the lady with the heavy blush and the frosted tips.

Unoriginal, but this question was at least more challenging than the first, and the judges got what they got: lots of dog answers.

I happened to love beagles. Our family had gotten a dog a couple years prior, an adorable beagle puppy that we'd named Kelly. I'd loved that dog with all my heart, but within two weeks she'd chewed up everything in the house—our socks, our underwear, the couch, the stove—so Dad didn't let us keep her. I naturally left out a lot of detail in my answer (that I'd once had a dog but my dad was a dog hater), because that wasn't endearing. I did, however, give a 500-word dissertation on how and why I would love to have a beagle. And I would name it Kelly Two.

My group of ten waited awkwardly, fidgeting on stage while the votes were tallied. Finally, the lady called a couple numbers. 67! Movin' on!

I turned on my heel and walked off the stage in my purple maxi, the word *Yes! Yes! Yes!* exploding in my head. My only thought was getting back up on that stage for the next round. I loved the thrill of the spotlight! Speaking into the little microphone. I even loved holding that paper plate. And the words were flowing like water! For the pet question, I practically had to be pulled off the stage with one of those vaudeville canes. I was on fire.

Thirty or so girls made it to the third round. We were getting down to the nitty-gritty, and for this question, you had to think on your feet and form a coherent, structured answer. The wheat was fixing to be separated from the chaff.

The lady spoke:

"Name anywhere in the world you'd like to visit, and why."

Boom. Canada. My sister Annie had just gotten back from Vancouver, British Columbia, where she'd gone for a school-sponsored choir trip or something, and I was completely stoked on Canada. It was the farthest any of the kids in our family had ever gone, and I thought Canada was the coolest place a person could possibly ever go. Canada may as well have been the moon. I had no idea it was only a four-hour drive away.

I spoke into the little microphone and let fly with an oral travelogue on Canada. I became the Canadian Ambassador for Tourism, rattling off population info, climate data, census stats, tourist destinations. I listed capital cities. Indigenous fauna. Famous Canadians. Dead Canadians. The audience felt like they were *in* Canada when I was done. You could smell the maple trees. Hear the roar of the hockey crowd!

Cane!

And I waited.

"Number 67."

I was going to get to do my poem!

The finalists were hustled backstage and hurriedly told that this was it: eight girls, eight speeches. We would recite our pieces one at a time, in the order in which we were lined up, and for this round, we each got to hold the microphone! A real microphone!

With the curtain closed, the organizers arranged us on stage. I was placed on the far side—stage left, audience's right—and would be the last to deliver my speech. We contestants shuffled and adjusted. "Arm's length apart!" our emcee whispered as the curtain opened and she walked backward offstage. "And don't trip over the cord!"

Again, I was faced with the sea of eyeballs; the hushed audience and judges.

Over the next few moments, I stood and listened to the other contestants' speeches, and became more and more anxious as the microphone moved down the line. My heart was pounding in my ears. The time had come, the moment we'd all prepared for.

Well, some of us anyway.

The girl beside me, number seven in line, geared up to speak, her plate and voice shaking.

"I, I, I like kittens, and butterflies, and, and, ice cream. And pizza," she said. "And I have a mom and a dad."

Silence.

Was that it?

This girl must have gotten past the first three rounds on guts and moxie, because it was obvious she had nothing prepared for the final. Maybe a big brother had told her she didn't need to bother memorizing a speech because she wasn't going to use it, and maybe she'd listened to him. The audience applauded courteously, feebly, and she handed me the mike, defeated and nearly in tears. It was sad—the poor thing. I was next!

I stepped forward with the microphone, giving the cord a fling to create some slack, and waited for the audience to focus on the last contestant.

Me.

I recited my "Pachycephalosaurus" poem, five delight-ful verses about the dinosaur with the long name and the small brain; the knobby cheeks and spiky nose. The zinger of a punch line at the end. My four weeks of practice had paid off. Not a misstep or hiccup.

I finished, and giggles and applause rose like steam from the audience. The poem was a hit—engaging, solidly delivered—and quite a piece for a person of my age and stature to deliver. But what made it all the more endearing was that as a third-grader, I could not pronounce my *R*'s. I was three-and-a-half feet tall, with my wonky teeth and Jan Brady drapery hair, delivering my dinosaur poem, and

I sounded like Elmer Fudd. Adorable! I should have had on an oversized felt hat and a pretend rifle slung over my shoulder. "*You wascally wabbit!*"

Our emcee called for a final round of applause, and we girls gazed out into the audience and bright lights, holding our plates as the curtain closed. It was over.

Behind the thick theater curtain, we were herded to the side of the stage. The lights were low, and the murmur of the waiting audience out front, a delicious hum. Activity became feverish for a moment or two as several assistants bustled about, then approached our emcee, waving pieces of paper in her face. Our silver-haired lady grabbed the papers, took a look, and walked briskly toward us. "Gather 'round, girls, gather 'round! We have a result!" she chirped.

We gathered 'round. Ms. Emcee was flushed and smiling. She drew us in with her eyes, and we formed a tighter circle. Her assistants smiled beside her as she held the papers to her ample chest and I glanced at my plate to remind myself of the number I wanted to hear.

"You are all little princesses," she said tenderly, "and you all did a tremendous job, but there can only be one winner."

Hushed tones. Eye contact with all. Dramatic pause.

"It's number 67," she said.

I looked at my plate.

I won. Holy crap, I won. Mom was gonna freak!

With the curtain still closed, the organizers pulled me toward the center of the stage and placed me on a throne (really just a big chair) and wrapped a huge red cape around my shoulders, meant to signify royalty, I guess. I was engulfed; this cape was the size of a catamaran sail. Someone handed me a dozen red roses, and posed the other finalists in a circle around me in preparation for the reveal.

I won.

I had won.

Tony!

The curtain opened, and I was announced as the winner for District 4. It was official; I was a princess. The lady with the big hair had said so.

I looked out into the auditorium at all the people, applauding and smiling. Through the bright lights, I found the faces of my sisters and my aunt, sitting in the fourth row—smiling and clapping. Laughing, gesturing and elbowing. Then I spotted Mom, who wasn't so much clapping or smiling, but more looking down at her lap. Shaking her head and rubbing her eyebrows. Maybe her eyebrows were itchy.

I couldn't stop smiling, and I also couldn't move. This cape weighed about a hundred pounds.

* * *

Directly after the princess competition, we drove downtown to the *Oregonian* building. The Rose Festival people had told Mom that the newspaper needed my picture for the morning edition. It was now after 10 p.m., and I was in downtown Portland! At a newspaper building, getting my picture taken!

My family and I followed a man with a camera into a big room full of desks and reporters and typewriters. I looked around in amazement; I'd never seen a sight like this: dozens of newspaper reporters hunched over their machines, pounding away on the keys. The decibel level was so high,

I had to raise my voice to ask the photographer a question. "Can I use one of the phones?"

"Sure, help yourself," he said.

I had to call home. I walked to an empty desk while the rest of my party waited, and dialed our number. Tony answered.

"Tony, guess what?!" I said, sticking my finger in my other ear.

"What," he said.

"I won!" I shouted above the clatter.

"You did not."

"I did too and I'm at the *Oregonian* right now getting my picture taken for the newspaper and I'm in the typing room and everybody's typing! Listen!"

I thrust my arm, and the phone, high into the air so Tony could hear the sound of thirty typewriters click-clacking away. There I was, in my purple maxi dress and mismatched barrettes, a black phone receiver in one hand and a bouquet of red roses in the other. Smiling through my oversized Chiclet tooth and gum pimple.

I held that receiver high, and moved it around like an oscillating fan.

Chapter Twenty-One

Rose Festival Grand Floral Parade, 1973.

The Junior Princess gig was three weeks of treats, excursions, gifts, and meals out. I ate more french fries in my twenty-one days as princess than I had in my previous nine years of life.

And the rumor I'd heard about the new clothes was true. We got three outfits in all: a beautiful custom-made gown made of yellow seersucker; a casual everyday outfit consisting of a white blouse and a pair of purple stretch bell-bottoms; and for events calling for a business-casual look, a skirt and jacket in an orange and pink combo, accessorized with a coordinating orange pom-pommed beret.

I owned a beret.

The job of a Junior Rose Festival Princess was easy: be adorable, attend events and sing songs (we learned three, one with choreography), and act as miniature, well-behaved ambassadors for Portland, the City of Roses. We curtsied at every turn.

One chaperone was assigned to every two princesses, and I loved mine. Sylvia was pretty and smelled like a soft perfume. And the silver-haired lady who emceed my tryout? That was Elaine, the head chaperone who, I learned, had emceed each princess competition. She was married to the president of the Rose Festival.

For each event, our parents dropped us at our designated meeting place (a bank in the Hollywood district), where our chaperones took over and drove us to our functions in fancy Rose Festival cars: cream-colored sedans with magnetic rose emblems attached to the doors.

We were constantly on the go.

We went to the beach and the zoo.

We visited the State Capitol and got our picture taken with the Governor.

We were invited to a luncheon on a sternwheeler by a women's group, and received special tours of Portland's Pittock Mansion and Franz Bakery. We rode floats in several citywide parades.

Each and every Rose Festival event was great fun, but when our chaperones told us one day near the end of our reign that they had a special surprise for us, told us it had all been arranged and were we ready to hear this, well, all other excursions seemed just another day at the office. Getting a slice of white bread with butter on it, bread that had come directly out of the gigantic oven at the Franz Bakery and was still warm and soft? Getting permission to pet the baby elephant at the Portland Zoo? Peanuts compared to what was coming.

We had just finished lunch at Farrell's Ice Cream Parlour, the famed Portland restaurant with the black-and-white checkerboard tile floors, soda fountain, and oversized gift-shop lollipops. Lunch at Farrell's was amazing—another burger with fries!—and the mood was festive. We girls chattered and laughed throughout the meal, and our chaperones were especially upbeat. They told us we'd get the surprise as soon as we left the restaurant, so after lunch, the eight of us stood outside the restaurant's doors with two of our ladies and waited for Elaine and Sylvia to pay the bill. We milled around on the sidewalk, full and happy, in our orange and pink mock business suits. While we waited, we checked out the gift we'd just received from our festival guardians: new autograph books, cream-colored as well and monogrammed with our names; mine misspelled, but still, another goodie. The Rose Festival people didn't miss a trick.

I asked Jeannette (District 7), my fellow princess and town-car mate, what she thought the surprise might be.

"I don't know," she said. "Maybe another outfit? Or a purse? A camera!" My new pal Jeannette Lopez was from the wrong side of the tracks, just like me, and we loved getting all the stuff. I had six siblings and wore hand-me-down underwear, and Jeannette lived with her two brothers and grandparents in a two-bedroom apartment. Every gift and trinket we received, we appreciated.

What was the surprise? we all wondered. We knew the Grand Floral parade, the culminating event of the Rose Festival, was right around the corner, and we knew we'd be meeting Betty White, the lady from *The Mary Tyler Moore Show*, who was this year's parade marshal.

Finally, Elaine and Sylvia joined us outside, laughing as

they pushed open the door. All four of the adult chaperones huddled together, whispering and giggling and carrying on. We princesses glanced at each other, puzzled. I thought for a second a few of the ladies might be drunk—they were usually so dignified.

Elaine broke from the group and called for our attention, while the other three women gathered beside and behind. All four faces were bright and smiling, but our lead chaperone, theatrical in general, was practically levitating. She waited until all eyes were on her. "Who's ready for the news?" she sang, palms in the air.

We are! Tell us! Tell us!

We inched closer, and I flashed back to the semicircle I'd stood in a few weeks ago with Elaine and seven different girls, and wondered if anyone else was having a déjà vu.

"We're going to a concert," Elaine said. "A very *special* concert, next Friday night, at the Civic Auditorium, downtown."

"The Civic Auditorium?" My fellow princesses turned to each other and nodded, big-eyed and knowing. "Downtown?"

"The Civic Auditorium?" I chimed in right along with them. I had no idea what or where that was.

"And that's not all. We have backstage passes," Elaine said, smiling so hard I thought she might split in two. She was drunk. She had to be.

"What concert? What concert?!" we shouted.

Elaine adored the dramatic pause.

"The Brady Bunch!"

* * *

I needed a moment.

Because what I thought I'd just heard her say was that we were going to see the Brady Bunch in concert and that we had backstage passes.

We princesses looked at each other again in disbelief, and the shrieking began. We grabbed hold of shoulders and elbows and jackets and jumped up and down like an eight-headed orange and pink rocket launcher. No wonder the chaperones had taken us outside; we were causing a scene. Traffic slowed on Weidler—drivers trying to figure out what was going on with this bouncing pastel blob of humanity in the Farrell's parking lot.

The Brady Bunch was huge. Friday night prime-time. Sure, the show was cooling off, and the Brady kids had taken to touring the country with a stage show full of unhip tunes and slapped-together dance routines, but they were still the Brady Bunch. Jeannette and I gained our composure, hugged the chaperones, and said goodbye to the gang. We got in our car to head to the bank for parent pickup.

"The Brady Bunch," Jeannette said, staring out the windshield. "We're gonna meet Bobby Brady."

We drove back in a daze.

The night of the show arrived. Mom drove me to the bank in Hollywood, and from there our chaperones took over and chauffeured us downtown in the Rose Festival sedans. We crossed the Broadway Bridge, and Jeannette and I gazed out the windows at the Willamette River and the city lights.

We parked on 4th Avenue and hurried past the Keller Fountain to the concert site. Our chaperones looked smart in their cream-colored dress suits, an official Rose Festival

broach pinned to their lapels, while the eight of us princesses were decked out in our orange skirts and pink blazers—
berets in place, white socks pulled smartly to the knees. We
arrived at the Civic Auditorium, Portland's fanciest concert
venue, and another first for me. We made our way into the
lobby along with the hundreds of other Brady Bunch fans,
and I gazed up at the beautiful high ceiling. Next we entered
the grand auditorium and I marveled at the plush chairs and
the balconies.

We found our seats, vibrating with excitement. Jeannette and I were the first to ask to use the facilities, and we
ran up the aisle of the dim auditorium and into the lobby. We remarked on the coat check ladies, the massive glass
front entrance, the ornate chandeliers. We speed-walked to
the restroom and looked at each other in disbelief. *Couches
in the bathroom!?*

We rushed back to our seats and settled in as the auditorium filled up. Ten minutes to showtime, the place was
packed.

Finally, the lights came down and the Brady kids were
introduced, jogging onstage for their first number in colorful
bellbottomed outfits; halter tops for the girls and wide-col-
lared dress shirts for the boys; each piece accessorized with
beaded fringe! I wished *I* had a halter top with beaded
fringe! The crowd went mad, and I couldn't believe what
was before me. My idols! The Brady Bunch. These were the
kids I watched on TV every single Friday night, and now I
was seeing them in person, singing and dancing in unison
(mostly), and interacting with the audience. I didn't blink
for five minutes.

Greg shined as the true star and unofficial leader on

stage. He introduced the numbers and bantered expertly with the audience, going on and on about Portland—how he loved the city, the concert hall, the amazing crowd—telling all the lies performers tell in the cities they visit. *What an audience! Great to be here! Portland, Seattle, Boise, New Delhi, wherever we are! Fantastic crowd!*

Greg and Marcia (Barry Williams and Maureen McCormick) were the main stars, but all six kids sang and danced and moved and grooved. They ran offstage for a costume change, and bounded back to sing and dance some more.

When the Bradys performed their big TV hit, "Sunshine Day", the place went elementary-school-kid berserk.

> *Everybody's smiling!*
> *Sunshine day!*
> *Everybody's laughing!*

This was a concert.

Finally, Greg quieted things down in preparation for the final few numbers, and took a moment to allow the audience to catch its collective breath. A stool appeared at the side of the stage, and he grabbed it and sauntered to center stage.

"Time to slow things down a bit," he said, as he swung the stool under his body in a fluid motion. "Time for me to dedicate the final song to one lucky little lady." Greg (Barry) was yet a teenager, but he worked the crowd like a seasoned lounge singer.

"On the count of three, I want every one of you to shout your name," he man-whispered. The audience was, of course, approximately ninety-eight percent female, and if you didn't count the moms and dads and chaperones, approximately one hundred percent under 13. We would have done anything he asked.

"One, two, three!" On Greg's cue, the place erupted. Every Lisa, Tammy, Rhonda and Karen screamed bloody murder, and every adult covered his or her ears. I shouted my name as loud as I could. I *so* wanted this dedication. I deserved it. I was the biggest Brady Bunch fan ever!

Working the prepubescent crowd into a G-rated frenzy, Greg repeated, "Louder, I can't hear you!" cupping his hand over his ear for effect. And again came the screaming. Finally, after a third time Greg apparently heard a name clearly enough that he was able to dedicate the song. To "Laura."

I didn't hear Laura. I heard Sherri, loud and clear! And so did everyone within a hundred-foot radius of my mouth. Laura must have been up towards the front.

The show ended. Time to go backstage! As the rest of the audience filed out of the auditorium, we princesses followed our chaperones down the aisle and toward the stage, against the flow of traffic. Adults and kids exiting the rows of seats eyed us hard, undoubtedly curious about what kind of troupe we were in that we were a) invited backstage to meet the Brady kids, and b) dressed like Easter eggs.

A silent man with an I.D. badge attached to his maroon jacket led us down a long, windowless corridor. We were going "backstage." We were entering the palace in *Oz*.

We were meeting the Brady Bunch.

The usher opened the door, revealing a large, elegantly lit high-ceilinged room, decorated in dark woods and plush red carpet. A grand piano sat in the corner, and fancy furniture occupied a sunken lounging area. And there they were: the Brady kids, in human form, standing under subdued, swanky lights, like gems in a jewelry case. They practically sparkled.

Our twelve-person Rose Festival party stood at the entrance, taking in the sight of Greg, Marcia, Jan, Peter, Bobby and Cindy, in their street clothes. It threw me to see Peter (Christopher Knight) in a leather jacket, and Jan (Eve Plumb) in massive bellbottoms and a frilly hippie top. Gone were the barrettes, draped hair, and octagonal wire-rimmed glasses. She was working hard to shake that *Jan* image.

We princesses stood frozen until our chaperones jolted us from our trance. They gathered us up and gave us the rundown: we would have just a short time with the Brady kids and we needed to make the most of it. We were allowed to ask for only two autographs; no time for all six. *Go. Go!*

Armed with our Rose Festival-issued autograph books, we were let loose in the room—no introductions, no receiving line—simply sprung free to approach whoever we wanted. Marcia! Greg! Bobby! Peter! Crap! I didn't know what to do. I'd never had a brush with greatness, and I didn't know how to approach a famous person. I barely knew how to approach a regular person!

I scanned the room again and decided to go for Greg and Marcia, Barry and Maureen, who were standing together at one side of the room. Most of the girls bolted for them, as they seemed the most welcoming, and I got in line. I finally made it to Marcia, and asked for her autograph. Marcia was a goddess. She spoke my name.

I looked up at Greg. "Could I have your autogr—"

"How'd you enjoy the show?" he said as he grabbed

my book and smiled that million-dollar smile. He signed his autograph, which, incidentally, was full of flair. Barry Williams. What a guy.

I turned and considered my next move. I'd been so focused on Greg and Marcia, I hadn't noticed what was taking place in our grand suite. Greg and Marcia had been popular draws at the beginning of this grocery grab, and Peter and Jan were right up there too, but now everyone had the same idea, and nearly every princess headed in the same direction: toward Bobby. Mike Lookinland. Bobby was cute—no Davy Jones, but cute—and the natural choice if any of us princesses had a romantic fantasy. He was closest to us in age, in the sixth or seventh grade compared to our third and fourth.

As I watched, the other girls closed in on Bobby. With autograph books open and pens thrust skyward, each princess gazed up, hoping for a lasting look or a small bit of extra attention from Bobby Brady. Something, anything she could take back to school on Monday morning.

I desperately wanted to talk to him, too, but I held back. I didn't know what I could possibly say to him to break the ice. I wasn't allowed to ask him for his autograph because I'd already reached my limit with Greg and Marcia, so that pickup line was out of the question.

Maybe I could say, "Hi, Bobby."

Well, I knew good and well his name wasn't Bobby. I couldn't call him Bobby! I'd heard that some stars got mad if you called them by their character names. And I couldn't call him by his real name, Mike, because that sounded even more ridiculous. We hadn't been introduced!

I watched as all the other princesses now completely

surrounded him, each one becoming bolder and louder, vying for his attention. These were the girls gutsy enough to talk to him, or too daft to know they shouldn't. I was neither gutsy nor daft. I was just scared. And time was running out.

I had an idea. I'd go through Cindy. Susan Olsen. Yes! Sweet little Cindy Brady with the lisp and the pigtails. Cindy would be my confidante; my bridge to Bobby.

I spotted her, standing alone, away from the autograph fracas. She leaned against the grand piano at the far edge of the red-carpeted room, doing her best Marlene Dietrich, still in full makeup. She looked bored, irritated, maybe a little standoffish, but I didn't let that deter me. She was Cindy Brady! Cindy was nice! We had a connection. I was the youngest girl in my family; she was the youngest in hers. We were both the number-six child! I thought I had a perfect question for her. A great conversation starter.

I adjusted my beret and walked right over, looking directly into the striking blue eyes of Cindy Brady.

"So, how old is Bobby?" I asked brightly.

Suddenly, I realized how much taller Cindy was than me. And older. And meaner.

She looked me up and down, from the top of my jaunty beret to the tips of my white Mary Janes, and with one elbow resting on the piano, she sneered—literally *sneered* at me—and said, "Why don't you go ask him yourself," tossing her head in Bobby's direction.

Well, that stung. It was a simple question, and probably one she'd heard about ten thousand times. What was her problem? There was actual contempt in her voice—even her cute little lisp was gone! Maybe she'd gotten some speech therapy during the show's hiatus.

I stood stunned into silence. I was certainly not prepared for a reaction like that, and I had no backup plan whatsoever. I removed my beret, did a slow one-eighty on the heel of my Mary Jane, and skulked back to the safety of the chaperones, whose faces were still plastered with smiles as they gawked at the most famous family in the country.

I stood with the ladies and watched as the other princesses clamored over Bobby, the entire pint-sized mob one step shy of tearing at his clothes. I held tight to my autograph book and beret until our meet-and-greet was over.

I never did get to talk to Bobby and I never did find out how old he was. I knew the answer, though: *too old for me.*

Our time was up with the Brady kids. Overall, the night had been excellent. I'd gotten to see the Brady kids live in concert. I'd gotten backstage. I'd gotten autographs. I'd had a conversation with Greg and Marcia Brady. And I'd spoken to Cindy Brady, learning a small piece of trivia that most kids in America would never know: Cindy Brady was a little B-I-T-C-H.

Excellent night.

Chapter Twenty-Two

I jumped out of the car and took off toward the house.

Dinnertime was long past, and the sun was low in the sky, shining sideways onto our front porch. I ran up the wide, painted concrete steps, and Mom followed with a bag of groceries.

As I got closer to the front door, I noticed something on the porch. Something shimmery. A bottle, poking out from the top of a brown paper bag.

The glass bottle and the liquid inside gleamed and glinted in the sunlight; the whole package sparkled like a jewel. Then I saw it: a tassel—a beautiful, fluffy, purple tassel, draped around the neck of the bottle.

A tassel! I loved tassels. A tassel would be the perfect addition to my collection of special things!—my small, square metal container I had dubbed my "collection box."

It was really an old recipe holder, but I had big plans for it; gems, seashells, thunder eggs. Currently my rusty little tin contained three items, none of which was a gem, a seashell, or a thunder egg. Currently, the best thing in my collection box was a stained and oversized cloth-covered button that I'd found in the basement under Mom's sewing machine.

I *needed* this tassel.

And there it hung, thick and luxurious—like a big, beautiful plum, ready to be plucked.

I bent down and grabbed the tassel. It was instinct: I saw something beautiful and purple, and I went for it. My hands were on it, it was mine, and suddenly, Mom was behind me. She cursed a quiet and clenched-toothed *"God-dammit,"* leaned over and yanked the tassel, the bottle—the entire bag—from my grasp. She stood up, and I watched the tassel disappear.

She could have the bottle; I didn't want it. I knew what it was. Alcohol for Dad. Most likely left on the porch by Grandma Min's husband, Grandpa Hank. Dad and Grandpa Hank were drinking buddies, and Mom didn't like it when Grandpa left Dad bottles of liquor.

She walked into the house with the groceries and the bottle, angry, and I never saw the tassel again.

I walked inside, mad too. At least for the next ten minutes or so. I wanted that tassel. Nobody else would have taken care of it like I would have, and I'm sure it went to waste.

Chapter Twenty-Three

Raleigh Hills lay in a part of the city we never ventured. We had no family or friends there, so when Mom put me and Andy in the car and drove—fifteen, twenty, twenty-five minutes—across the Willamette River, up into the west hills, well, I thought we were entering a foreign land: a beautiful neighborhood with a forest-like feel; homes with manicured lawns and big garages. Wide, clean streets, free of the giant meandering motor oil stains common in our Southeast Portland neighborhood. This area was *nice*. Raleigh Hills may as well have been Beverly Hills.

Plunked in the middle of this leafy hamlet was Raleigh Hills Clinic, where Dad was going to live for the next thirty days. Tony told me all about Raleigh Hills: that people came here to stop drinking when they couldn't stop on their own; that they took medicine that made them sick if they drank alcohol. After the medicine, they were forced to drink alcoholic drink after warm alcoholic drink, then sit in a chair with an attached trough and throw up until they couldn't throw up anymore. After that, they drank and threw up some more. After all that throwing up, they moved to the next step, which was the dry heaves. The next day, they woke up with a hangover and did it all over again.

The treatment at Raleigh Hills was something called "aversion therapy," which sounded like a fancy term for *vomit-based torture*. If it was me, I would have taken the easy way out and just stopped drinking.

Mom parked on the street in front and led me and Andy up a cement path toward the clinic doors. A steady, misty rain fell.

"Quick, kids, let's go," she said, and pulled us by our hands to the doors. We stepped inside the clinic, and I looked around. I saw no nurses' station or information desk, only a long hallway with uniformly-spaced doors on either side. This place seemed more like an office building or an old school, only with weirder smells. Mom found a man in a windowless office and had a few quiet words with him, then took our hands again. We walked slowly down the empty, echoey hallway, and I slid the fingers of my free hand along the bumpy green-painted walls.

We came to a large, rectangular room where the patients stayed and I paused at the doorway. I saw two rows of beds, one on either side of the room, and felt like I'd stepped into a *Madeline* book, only it wasn't children in their pajamas and beds, but grown men. Twenty or thirty of them, lounging around during what I guessed were visiting hours, but from what I could tell, Mom and Andy and I were the only visitors there.

Some of the men turned our way and smiled, some chatted quietly with each other, and a few others looked tired and sick. I wondered if all of them were like my dad: one type of person when they were sober, and another when they were drunk.

I spotted Dad in his bed, wearing a thin blue hospital gown and leaning against his headboard. My dad, the tall, stern disciplinarian who never mistreated me in particular, but who I feared, looked different. Nervous. Scared? I couldn't tell. I'd never seen my dad look scared. I'd also never seen him sitting up in a bed and doing nothing, ever.

His legs were bare and he held his knees to his chest. He looked small.

Mom let go of my hand, and Andy and I went to Dad. He leaned over to give me a hug. "How ya doing, sweetie?"

"Fine," I said. Dad tried to look happy, and he smiled at me and Andy, but I could tell it was a fake smile. He was trying too hard, and he was shaking.

He didn't look at Mom at all.

Chapter Twenty-Four

It was a dark and stormy night. No, really, it was.

I sat alone in our basement watching my favorite show as the wind blew and the rain *tat-tatted* against the window in our TV room.

It was quiet—just me and the TV—rare for a Friday night. I had no one to argue with over who got the best seat or what we were going to watch. Not that we had a lot of choices for seats *or* channels. We had one couch, and a total of four TV channels, five if you counted the one that stunk: Channel 10, Public Broadcasting, which I did not. The only things worth watching on Channel 10 were *Electric Company*, and maybe *Zoom*. On a Friday night, Channel 10 would have been airing some idiotic British drama about a chubby chambermaid who solves the weekly village murder. Crumpets and tea and bumbling chimney-sweep sidekicks; pewter gravy boats as murder weapons. No, my Friday night was reserved for *The Brady Bunch*, still the best show ever, and the best thirty minutes of my week.

The Brady Bunch ended, and I shifted on the couch and watched whatever came on after that. *The Odd Couple. Room 222.* I came out of my TV trance and wondered why it was so quiet. Nobody had come downstairs in ages, and I hadn't heard any footsteps or talking upstairs. Actually, I hadn't heard much of anything for quite a while. The only sounds were the icy rain hitting the lone downstairs window, and periodic gusts of wind rattling the glass. Outside it was pitch black—an awful night. And a weird night, but things were weird in general.

Dad had moved out a few months prior, maybe for good this time, but I wasn't a hundred percent sure; he'd moved out before, and Mom and Dad didn't talk directly to me about a divorce. They didn't schedule the "we still love you kids, but can't stand each other," talk. I had to figure things out on my own.

And I was pretty sure I had: the day I came home from school and seventy percent of the living room furniture was gone. Dad had taken it, even our huge sleeper couch. This time he *must* have been serious—Dad didn't go around moving two-ton hide-a-beds for effect. What remained in the living room were a crummy couch and old rocking chair we'd gotten from Grandma Min, which Mom supplemented with a side table and a few wooden apple crates.

Mom was overwhelmed. A two-parent household was a thing of the past, and maintaining a big house and yard were her sole responsibilities, in addition to the relentless task of preparing dinner every night for seven kids, four of them teenagers.

My older siblings were scattering to the breeze, and Mom had told us younger kids we'd be leaving Our Lady of Sorrows to go to the public school in our neighborhood, and that she'd be starting a job at a coffee shop working an off-shift.

I wasn't entirely neglected, but a few small luxuries I'd taken for granted before, like being driven to appointments or having my laundry done on any kind of a regular basis were also becoming memories. I'd started walking the six blocks to our dentist's office when I needed a filling or broke a molar, and if I wanted clean clothes, I was on my own. "You can reach the dials now, time to learn how to do your washing," Mom had said. Actually, I couldn't reach the dials, I had to use a footstool.

Things were weird all right. And this house was too quiet.

I moved down to the rug on the floor of the TV room and leaned against the couch. I flipped onto my belly. It was 9:30 and I hadn't seen anyone since *The Brady Bunch* had come on at 8:00. I scooted over to the TV, turned the volume down, and listened for noises upstairs. Still nothing.

I trotted upstairs and into the kitchen. "Mom?" I called, walking from the kitchen to the dining and living rooms. All empty.

"Mom?!"

Silence.

"Terri?!

"Mitzi?

"Tony?! Joe?!"

Where was everybody? Where was Annie? What about Andy?

I crossed the dining room to the hallway leading to the staircase to our second floor, and stood at the base of the steps. I stayed put at the bottom and called again. "MOM!"

I thought about walking up to see if someone was asleep in one of the bedrooms, but decided against it. I was not about to go upstairs alone, not with that gigantic closet at the top of the landing. A family of murderers could be camped out in there. I didn't like to go past that closet in the middle of the day, when everybody was home! I sure wasn't going to go up there on a black, rainy night like this.

I called again. "Anybody here?!"

I stood at the bottom of the staircase and took in the stillness: the dim hallway behind me, the two bedrooms, the bathroom—every door open and every room glaringly empty. I heard something at that moment that I rarely heard in this house: total silence.

This couldn't be. I had six siblings and a mom. I was cared for. I may have recently had to walk across four lanes of traffic on Powell Boulevard, by myself and without benefit of a crosswalk in order to get to my last dentist appointment, and I had to be the only ten-year-old on my block who knew to separate colors from whites, but I was never left alone in the house at night. I could not have been left alone.

I was alone. No one had even said goodbye.

I walked from the stairs back to the living room and stood. I spoke a word or two out loud to try to make myself feel less alone, but that made the house feel emptier than before.

Where was Mom? She wouldn't have left me! She must have assigned someone to take care of me before she'd gone out. She'd been acting different lately, preoccupied, sure, but leaving me unsupervised wasn't like her at all. Surely she'd left Mitzi or Terri or Tony in charge. Mitzi must have left, thinking Terri or Tony was still home. Terri must have gone out, assuming Mitzi or Tony was taking care of me. Any number of combinations could have taken place, but the fact was, I had been forgotten, abandoned. My worst fear.

I'd had nightmares in the past, dreams of being left alone in our big house, walking through our living room and opening the front door to darkness and ghouls and creepy feelings, and now it had come true.

I didn't know what to do. I didn't even know where to stand.

I couldn't go upstairs, and no way was I going back downstairs to the TV room—that meant walking down the open staircase to the empty basement. I'd had nightmares about that staircase too: visions of shriveled witch hands reaching out between the slats of the stairs and grabbing at my feet as I descended. And directly behind the staircase, rumbling to life every eight minutes like a living, breathing creature, sat our gigantic oil furnace. Next to *it* was the dark, musty storage alcove where Mom kept her canned goods, stacked on homemade wooden shelves. I could easily be killed in my own house, shoved in the corner of the storage space and forgotten, next to Mom's pickled green beans, also forgotten.

I had no choice but to call Dad at his new house in Milwaukie. I knew he'd be mad. Dad didn't like this kind of thing: mistakes and mess-ups and inconveniences. But I didn't know where Mom was; I didn't know where anyone was. If Vicki still lived down the street, I could have called her and her mom Bonni would have taken care of me. But the Derflers had moved away. There was no one else.

I dialed Dad's new number and he picked up. I opened my mouth to speak, and instead started to cry. I blurted out that I'd been left alone. He asked where Mom was. I said I didn't know. He asked where everyone else was, and I said I didn't know.

I heard him exhale. "I'll be there as soon as I can," he said.

I was right, he was mad.

"And you'll need to let me in."

Since he'd moved out months ago, Dad hadn't set foot inside the house. He didn't even park in front to pick me and Andy up for our Wednesday night visits. "Too many memories," he said. At 5:30 on Wednesday nights, Andy and I, sometimes a few of our older siblings, walked out the back door and down the alley to the corner where Dad waited for us in his idling Oldsmobile.

Dad wouldn't make me walk to the corner tonight. He was coming to the door.

I hung up the phone and sat in the quiet living room, listening to the icy rain pelting the windows until he arrived about thirty minutes later. He knocked, and I went to the door to let him in.

Dad stepped inside, wearing his dark brown raincoat and puffing on his pipe, and a stream of cold air followed him in. He said hello and not much else, and strode from the foyer to the main living area, like he'd done a thousand times before. This time, though, he seemed out of place. I kept quiet so he wouldn't have any reason to get angrier than he already was.

I stood beside him as he took deep breaths and surveyed the room in silence—the borrowed couch, the spindly rocking chair—resting his eyes on everything: the fireplace where he'd stood every Christmas Eve and waited for the seven of us to come racing down the stairs after we'd heard the sound of Santa's bells; the dining room where we'd eaten so many Thanksgiving meals. It was at this house that he'd turned the unfinished upstairs space into a huge bedroom for us girls, and installed an intercom on all floors so we could communicate with him and Mom in case of an emergency. It was at this house that Dad had built his kids a two-story playhouse in the backyard.

Dad loved this house and he missed us kids. I think he may have still loved Mom, too.

I followed him as he did a walk-through of the rest of the house, turning on every light and peering into every bedroom. Upstairs, downstairs. I'd left the TV on and he clicked it off. We headed back up to the main level.

In the kitchen, Dad refilled his pipe and pulled his silver lighter from his coat pocket. He held the pipe in his mouth, puffing softly as he opened a few of the kitchen cupboards. He walked into the living room, puffing and puffing, and stopped one last time.

After being gone so many months, I suppose he was checking things out. Seeing how the family was doing without him here. Had things fallen into disrepair? Were there signs of another man? Could he take that end table? What he was looking for, I didn't know.

"Let's get your coat," he said.

It was raining hard when we got in the car, but I wasn't scared anymore; I was safe with Dad. I kept quiet on the drive to his house on Sherrett Street, trying not to be any more trouble. He was still mad at me when we got there, but he made me a hot chocolate.

Chapter Twenty-Five

Me and Mom.

It was official: Dad was gone and Mom was a single mother of seven kids, all under the age of seventeen. She had her part-time job at the coffee shop down on 39th and Powell, and still did all the shopping and cooking, even though sometimes all we had for dinner was white rice with cinnamon and sugar.

Laundry piled up in the basement and the car broke down, but even so, Mom had a social life. Aunt Billie came over all the time now that Dad was gone, and she and Mom joined a bowling team. I didn't know it, but my mom was a pretty good bowler.

Mom started hanging out with a neighbor named Bobbie, too. Bobbie, a Janis Joplin look-alike, was bold and brassy, with a big voice and a big head of brown, wavy hair. She and Mom had always been friendly, but now that they were both single mothers with a bunch of kids, they had even more in common. They liked to go down to the neighborhood tavern on Division and shoot pool. Sometimes they drank wine and played cards or cribbage at our house, and when Bobbie was over, the volume level increased: Linda Ronstadt played on the stereo, Mom laughed, and I heard swear words and talk about men being jerks.

Bobbie lived across the street with her four kids in a house nearly identical to ours in size and structure: Old Portland style with two stories, a big front porch and picture window facing the street. I'd been in that house lots of times, playing with Bobbie's daughter Missy, who was in the same grade as me. It was a regular house on our regular residential street.

For some reason, Bobbie and her kids moved out of that house, and soon after, men started moving in. Men with no furniture and no moving vans. No wives or girlfriends or children.

Sometimes the men hung out on the porch, talking and smoking. They came and went at different hours of the day. They didn't appear to be related, but were similar in complexion, with dark hair and eyes.

Soon, a sign appeared on the front of the house—small, wooden and handmade, right next to the house number. The sign read "NARA." We learned that NARA stood for "Native American Rehabilitation Association."

Rehab for Native Americans.

A halfway house for alcoholic Native Americans.

We weren't familiar with NARA or halfway houses, but we were familiar with alcoholic Native Americans.

We called them drunk Indians.

Mom came from a huge family of Native Americans—a South Dakota Sioux tribe—and her mother, Grandma Min, was one of nine girls. Mom had about a thousand cousins, and so many aunts and uncles that I couldn't name them all. With a family this large, we had our share of alcoholic Native Americans, and Mom had heard stories of them her whole life. I'd heard them, too. Our family members didn't pass down the native Lakota language, or legends of how the crow came to be black, but they did pass down tales of our drunken relatives.

"Did you hear about cousin Leland?" my great-aunt Eve asked Mom at a family gathering. "He walked out into the street with no bottoms on the other night. Neighbors called the cops. Damn drunk Indian."

Aunt Billie called Mom one Sunday afternoon. "Anyone tell you about Uncle Robert? He got hauled off for shooting his neighbor in the leg with a BB gun last night. I guess they were playing darts in the garage and he thought his neighbor was cheating. Drunk Indian."

Mom drank a bit, but was most definitely *not* a drunk Indian. She *was,* however, completely familiar with and accustomed to them—and now there was a whole halfway-houseful, living a hundred feet away.

His name was Wilson. Wilson was good-looking, with thick black hair, and built like a pillar you might see supporting a small-town City Hall. The relationship started out with a friendly *hello* here and there. Wilson would smile and wave as Mom brought groceries in on a Saturday morning, or walk across the street and chat while she pulled weeds in the front yard. They began dating. Wilson paid Mom lots of attention and bought her things she liked: houseplants and little antiques; ivory combs and jewelry boxes. He helped fix her car. Wilson didn't pay much attention to us kids, however, and over the course of their six-month courtship, I don't think he ever learned all of our names.

Mom and Wilson spent time at our house, or at the neighborhood tavern playing pool. Sometimes Bobbie or Aunt Billie joined.

One night, after pool and beers with Mom, Wilson drove the two of them home from the tavern. As he came down Powell and was almost to our street, he saw flashing lights behind him. He may have had more to drink than Mom; he'd definitely been in more trouble with the law, and he panicked. Mom would later tell us that when he pulled over for the cop, he jammed the car into park and traded places with her; picking her up like a ragdoll and plunking her into the driver's seat, leaving her stunned and behind the wheel.

"I'm sure the cop noticed," Mom would say. "There's no way he couldn't have." She ended up getting a ticket for Wilson's bad driving, but she eventually forgave him.

A Saturday night in late November rolled around, and Bobbie was over, doing Mom's makeup and hair, experimenting with a "cascade," a flowy, clip-on hair extension. A big green jug of wine sat on the kitchen counter as Bobbie— loud, funny Bobbie, in her bellbottoms and clogs—played with Mom's black hair like a little girl playing with a Barbie doll. While drinking and smoking.

She teased and combed and fluffed Mom's hair as a cigarette burned in a foil ashtray a few feet away.

Mom sat on a stool at the kitchen table, sipping her glass of wine, and I came in to say goodnight. "How does my hair look, honey?" she asked.

"Pretty good," I said. Mom looked different with makeup on and her hair done. She rarely did either.

"I think she looks great!" Bobbie said, and played with Mom's hair some more. "Audrey, you look great."

I said goodnight and walked out of the kitchen.

"Happy birthday tomorrow, sweetie!" Mom called. "We'll make a cake."

My birthday!

At around midnight, I woke to shouting coming from downstairs, and I sat up in bed. I realized I was alone in the room I shared with my sisters, so I ran downstairs to see what all the commotion was.

Everyone was up.

I spotted Wilson standing in the small square foyer of our house. Dressed in Levis and a snug white T-shirt, he stood in front of Mom, and they were arguing about something; raising their voices. Bobbie stood at Mom's side, and she shouted at Wilson, too. Tony and Joe stood a few feet away in the living room, shivering in T-shirts and shorts. I crossed my arms over my chest as cold air poured through the open front door. I went to Annie and we stood with our backs against the dining room wall, watching the adults.

Mom yelled at Wilson. "I said, you need to get out!"

"Not until I get an answer," Wilson slurred. "Who's here? What's going on?" He had a cast on his lower leg, the kind with a big glob of rubber on the bottom for traction, and his jeans were slit to his knee to make room. "You havin' a party without me?"

"Keep your voice down!" Mom said. "You're waking everybody up! And no, we're not."

"Wilson, you need to get out of here," Bobbie said.

"Tell me who's here," Wilson said again, and moved closer to Mom.

"There's nobody here, I told you that," Mom said. She put her hands on his chest. "Now get out! You're drunk. Get out!"

"Wilson, you need to leave or I'm going to call the police," Bobbie said. She went to put her hand on his shoulder to steer him toward the door, but he pushed her away and she stumbled. Wilson grabbed Mom's chin with his left hand. "Who's here?" he said.

"There's no one here, Wilson, just us!" Mom said. He squeezed her chin so hard she could barely speak. "Let go of me!"

"Let go of her!" Tony said, and he took a step toward the foyer, just as Wilson spread his legs to adjust his balance on the rubbery cast and punched my mom in the face with his huge fist.

Bobbie jumped on him. "Stop it!"

"Get off her!" Tony yelled as he, Joe, and Bobbie pulled at Wilson, who acted like he didn't feel or hear a thing. He punched Mom in the face again and Tony ran out of the room.

"You're havin' a party without me!" Wilson said. "Aren't you!" Mom started to answer, but he hit her again.

"Call the cops," Bobbie said over her shoulder as she and Joe hung on to Wilson and tried to help Mom.

Terri ran the few steps to the dining room and picked up the phone. She dialed zero in the dim light, but Wilson saw. "Hang up the phone!" he boomed, keeping a hold of Mom. "Hang up the goddamn phone!" he yelled again, pointing at

Terri just as she reached someone at the other end.

"Never mind, never mind," Terri said meekly into the receiver, and hung up.

Tony had run downstairs and come back with a bat, and Bobbie took it from him.

"Wilson, stop it! Stop!" she said, as he tightened his grip on Mom. Bobbie held the bat above her head and aimed it at him, but she didn't use it. *Hit him!* I screamed in my head.

Hit him!

Annie and I stood frozen against the dining room wall, unable to do or say anything. Wilson had Mom pinned against the wall in the foyer and he hit her again. She tried to shield her face with her elbows.

Hit him, Bobbie!

She lowered the bat.

Bobbie and Tony and Joe fought with Wilson, and were finally able to get him off Mom, long enough for her to run through the living and dining room toward the kitchen and back door. Wilson shook them off and ran, and even on a cast he was quick. He caught Mom by the back of her shirt before she reached the kitchen doorway. He turned her around, held her steady and punched her in the face one, two, three more times.

Somebody do something!

He pulled Mom through the living room and into the foyer again. Bobbie and my brothers tried again to get him to let go of Mom, but he was just too powerful, and too drunk. Mom put her elbows in front of her face, and through her arms said, "Wilson, please stop! There's no one here. Please!"

The door was still open, and cold, damp air poured into the house. The seven of us kids stood around the room, silent. Wilson took a few breaths and loosened his hold.

Bobbie moved in front of Mom, facing Wilson.

"There's no one else here, Wilson! It's just me and Audrey," she said, out of breath. "No one else."

He looked at Bobbie, then around the room at us kids. His eyes were the exact color of his face: blood red. He looked back at Mom. Her face was battered and starting to swell, and things seemed to register with him. The house was silent. Maybe there wasn't anyone else here.

He paused a second, and took my mom's face in his hands. "I'm sorry! I'm sorry! I love you!" he said gruffly. Then he kissed her hard on the lips, pushed her face away, and hobbled out the front door. Bobbie closed the door and locked it behind him.

"Jesus, Audrey, are you all right?" she said.

She helped Mom to the living room couch, and Terri ran to the kitchen to get a bag of ice. Mom sat down and touched her face. Two huge lumps were forming on her forehead, and her eyes were puffy and scraped. Her lip was bleeding.

"I'm OK. I'm OK," Mom said.

She wasn't OK.

* * *

Terri called the operator again, and a short while later, two cops showed up. Bobbie walked Mom out to the front porch to talk to them, and I peeked through the front door.

I saw the back of one cop, and another with a notepad in his hands. Mom stood in the cold in just a T-shirt and jeans, and held the ice to her head. She let Bobbie do most of the talking.

"I grabbed that bat and I was going to hit him over the head with it," she told the cop. She puffed hard on a cigarette. "But I knew I'd kill him… I knew I'd kill him."

You should have, I thought to myself.

The police left, and Mom and Bobbie came back in the house.

My brothers and sisters and I sat in the living room—on the couch, on the floor—scared and shaken, and Bobbie sat in the rocking chair, chain-smoking.

"He thought a party was going on without him," Bobbie said, "all because your Mom had her hair fixed up. It was all because of that damn cascade." She took another long drag of her cigarette.

I sat next to Mom as she rested on the couch, not saying much. The lumps above her eyes were huge, and the rest of her face was bruised and battered. She looked awful, more sad than anything, but hadn't cried. Of course. Mom never cried.

"Well, this really ruined your birthday, didn't it, sweetie," she said to me. She was trying to make light of things, like she always did. *This too shall pass* was one of her mottos.

I'd forgotten it was my birthday. Mom smiled and pulled me in for a hug, and I burst into silent tears. She stroked my hair with one hand and held the ice with the other.

"Oh, yeah, happy birthday, Sher," I heard one or two

of my siblings say. I kept my face buried in Mom's shoulder.

We drove south later that morning, to Salem or Eugene or Roseburg, to stay with one of Mom's cousins for a few days, and to hide from Wilson. We never did make the cake.

And I never saw Wilson again.

Chapter Twenty-Six

I got down to the corner first, and hopped in the car with Dad. Andy was a few minutes behind.

"I'm learning lines to my play, want to hear?" I asked Dad. I'd been rehearsing for the play that my class was going to perform for the other fourth-graders at my new school. I had the part of the pioneer schoolteacher, Miss Jenkins, who, when a bad guy bursts into the schoolhouse and holds the class hostage after he's stolen a bunch of horses, has the wherewithal to lower the flag to half-mast, thus alerting the town sheriff and saving the day! It was a lively melodrama with a righteous ending, and I had a big part and lots of lines. I was good at memorizing stuff.

"OK, sure," Dad said. He'd been sitting in his car at the end of the block with the engine running, waiting for me and Andy to meet him for our Wednesday night sleepover.

Dad relaxed behind the wheel of the Olds, still in his suit and tie from work, and with a thermos of coffee in his hand. He drank coffee from morning 'til night. I got the script out of my book bag and began reading my lines.

A year ago, Dad probably wouldn't have had the patience to listen to me run lines. He would have been uptight and busy and told me to get one of my sisters to listen.

But over the past year, things had changed. The treatment at Raleigh Hills had worked for Dad and he'd stopped drinking. He'd moved out of the house, and the awful fighting between him and Mom had stopped. Actually, so had communication of any kind; they didn't speak. We'd been taken out of Catholic school and hardly ever went to church anymore. I wasn't thrilled that my parents had split up, but there was an upside: a peaceful household, and no more nuns.

We were all adjusting to a new normal, and with Dad sober now, we were seeing a different side of his personality: a pleasant, mellow side. He no longer freaked out when somebody left a cupboard door open. He allowed us to watch almost anything we wanted on TV. He allowed us to hum. He'd even started listening to popular music himself. He liked "Radar Love" by Golden Earring. He knew the words!

Dad had always smoked a pipe, and I never minded the sweet, nutty scent of his Borkum Riff, but now on occasion, I noticed a strange smell when I got in the car on Wednesday nights. And lately, I'd seen Dad close the curtains at his new house on Sherrett Street and roll a homemade cigarette.

My dad was now a pot-smoker.

"Coffee beans come from the ground, and so does

marijuana," Dad had said one night as Andy and I worked a jigsaw puzzle at the kitchen table and he toked away. I'd never known him to be much of a naturalist, but whatever; I'd take a relaxed, smiling, M&M-swilling Dad over the binge-drinking, belligerent, meat-throwing one of a couple years ago, any day.

I worked on my script as Dad pulled a skinny cigarette from the inside pocket of his suit jacket. He flipped open the top of his fancy silver lighter and lit up. He cracked his window, and the thick, smelly smoke wafted about as I read my lines and we waited for my little brother.

I asked Dad to read the part of the sheriff, and offered him my script. His hands were full, and as he reached for my papers, he offered it to me. The joint, that is. Held it right in front of my face.

What was going on here? Was my dad, this forty-year-old, strait-laced salesman—the person sitting next to me wearing a navy sport coat and wing-tipped shoes—passing his ten-year-old daughter a joint?

A test. That was it! Dad always gave me things to do that were slightly beyond my capabilities or age-appropriateness. Recently, he'd asked me to sharpen his good knives with his electric sharpener, and barely gave me any instruction. About a month ago, he'd had me carry a box of broken mason jars out to the garbage. "Be careful, don't cut yourself," was all he'd said, and handed me the box. Dad challenged me: I needed to figure out a way to open the lid of the garbage can and dump the broken glass without spilling it all over the sidewalk or slicing my fingers. I needed to concentrate, problem-solve. Figure things out on my own. His offering me the joint must be another way he would measure my capabilities—my maturity.

Or maybe it was similar to an Italian father offering his child her first drink of wine at the family's holiday dinner. Only this was a doobie and we were sitting in a 1970 Oldsmobile at the end of a dark alley on a residential side street.

I was curious, and safe with Dad. He would never knowingly offer me anything harmful, so I took the pinny little thing in my fingers and took a drag like I knew what I was doing.

Yuck! This was horrible! And it burned my throat! I was a kid—still in elementary school! I watched cartoons on Saturday mornings. I didn't even own a bra. Why was I smoking pot?!

I coughed and hacked.

Dad dropped the small stack of papers and quickly took the joint back. "Oh, gosh, maybe we shouldn't have done that," he said.

We? What's this "we"?

"You OK, honey?" he asked.

"Yeah, I'm OK," I said, bent over and sputtering. "Do you have any water?" I coughed some more and smacked my lips together, trying to understand this horrid taste in my mouth. *Yuck, yuck, yuck!* "How can you smoke this!?" I said.

Dad apologized again and again as he tried to tidy the items in his lap—the script, his thermos, his lighter—while keeping hold of the joint. He stifled a laugh.

I took the script back and breathed deep, in and out—*I just smoked pot!*—and looked over at him as he took another puff. *Geez, Dad!* He glanced my way with another apologetic look, holding in the smoke. Then he blew it out and up, toward the crack of the window.

"That was a mistake, sweetie. I'm really sorry," he said.

"I'm fine," I said. It was no big deal. "But I'm never going to smoke pot again!"

"Well, good," he said. "You don't have to." He laughed again, and I did, too.

Dad took the joint and snuffed it out with his fingertips, carefully placing what was left in a container. "I know I don't need to mention that we probably shouldn't tell Mom about this," he said as he tucked the container back into his jacket pocket.

I shook my head no, still catching my breath. Mom's people may have smoked the peace pipe a century ago, but currently it wasn't legal, and I knew that.

My little brother finally got to the car, and we took off for Sherrett Street. First, though, I asked Dad to stop at the Plaid Pantry on Foster so I could get a Pepsi and a Milky Way. I needed to get this horrible taste out of my mouth.

Chapter Twenty-Seven

"Pew! It smells like a cave down here," I said as I walked down the steep wooden stairs.

We didn't go downstairs very often at Dad's; there was nothing to do or see. The only things in the basement were the water heater and the furnace, but he told me and Andy to follow him anyway. Dad carried a leather pouch, a couple of magazines and a hammer, so I figured we were in for a chore or a lesson. Dad was always trying to teach us something.

"Yeah, it does kind of smell, doesn't it," he said, as he whistled one of his favorite tunes—"Strangers in the Night"—and hit the light switch at the bottom of the steps with his elbow. The room lit up with a trio of naked bulbs hanging in an unadorned light fixture.

The basement was small and dank, and the floor, cement—no tile or carpet. The walls were unfinished too, made of a loose concrete. I found a ballpoint pen on the floor near some paint buckets and poked at the crumbly wall until some of the gravel fell to the ground.

"Dad," I said over my shoulder, "OK if I mess up this wall?"

"Sure, you can't hurt it," he said between whistles. He was busy doing something at his makeshift workbench: an old table where he kept things like paint cans and turpentine and repurposed pickle jars full of nuts and bolts and nails.

"What are we doing, Dad?" I asked, and looked around for more hints as to what he had planned to enrich our minds.

Dad taught as he went, showing us his way to perform the most mundane tasks, from using a funnel to refill the liquid dish soap, to getting the last bit of peanut butter out of the jar. What could he possibly teach us in the basement? How to adjust the temperature on the water heater? Check the air ducts?

At the workbench, he opened his leather pouch. "I got a new gun today, and we're gonna see how she works," he said, pulling a small pistol out of his bag. "How about some target shooting?"

I turned and looked at Andy. *Shoot guns?* We weren't gun people. Dad liked to fish, but he wasn't a hunter, and I'd never seen him with a gun. I walked over and looked at it. It was small, with a short barrel and a curvy wooden handle, and the whole thing fit easily in his palm. Dad turned from me so I could still see it, but so the barrel pointed away.

He set the gun down on the table, humming as he tore a few pages from his boring *Time* and *Newsweek* magazines.

"Don't touch the gun," he said, then grabbed his hammer and a few small nails and walked from the workbench to the gravel wall. Pebbles dribbled to the floor as Dad gently nailed a page from the magazine to the wall. It was a picture; a headshot of a man in a suit and tie.

"That's the President!" I said. "President Nixon!"

I'd seen his picture before, lots of times, and my teacher had brought his name up in class not too long ago. She'd mentioned the word *Watergate*, and talked about some dumb thing going on with President Nixon and a few other people. I hadn't understood any of it, and didn't care to. The biggest news in my world was that Cousin Oliver had joined the cast of *The Brady Bunch*, and the show was getting stupid.

"That's right," Dad replied, pulling a small nail out of his mouth and tapping another photo into the wall. "And this is the Vice President, Spiro Agnew." A few more bits of gravel fell, but Dad didn't care. He was in a forgiving mood.

"*Completing zee line-up ahh Haldeman and Ehrlichman*," he said with the fake German accent he used to make us laugh. I took Dad's word for it on those two; I'd never heard of them. He took a look at his four photos arranged in a nice orderly line, then turned from the wall and walked back to his work table. He picked up the gun and told me and Andy it was a twenty-two, offering us a thirty-second talk on firearm safety. "Keep it pointed down. Never, and I mean *never* point it at anyone, not even as a joke, got it?"

"We got it!" Andy and I chorused.

"OK, well, let's have some fun then and get to shooting. And it might be best if you didn't tell your mother."

He handed me the pistol, and it was ten times heavier than any toy gun I'd ever held. *A real gun!* "Stand back, son," he said to Andy, directing him to a safe spot. "Your turn first, Sher."

I stood at the far wall, faced the magazine photos, and raised the gun. I looked down the small barrel. I still hadn't mastered the art of closing one eye—I was pretty sure I never would—so I put my left hand over my left eye and aimed. I went for Nixon first. He seemed the logical choice, like the top prize at a carnival game. I pulled the trigger. *Pop!* My arm jolted and my body jerked. "Wow!" I said, and giggled. I pointed the gun down and looked at the wall where I'd missed the photos by a few feet.

I glanced at Dad and he smiled. "Try again. You're doing fine," he said.

I shrugged. "OK, if you say so."

I pulled the trigger again, and again I missed. "Dang!"

I pulled again, and *pop!*—this one hit. Nixon's jowl exploded as the bullet embedded in the gravel wall behind it.

"Yes!" I said. "Got him!" I moved on to the other guy, the gray-haired one with the big forehead and the weird name. Spiro Agnew. I hit him first try. Right in the forehead. Then again. In the forehead. *This was getting easy.*

I shot until my bullets were gone.

"That's a nice job," Dad said as he took the gun from me and reloaded. He let me have another round, coaching me as I went along, and when I was finished, he prepped the gun for Andy. Andy shot and shot, filling the photos with holes. *Pop, pop, pop!*

"This is cool!" Andy said.

When Andy had had his fill, he handed the gun to Dad.

"Nice work, both of you," Dad said, smiling and nodding. "Now let me show you how it's done." He smacked the gun open and reloaded, humming "Born Free"—another one of his standbys. He stopped humming and turned to face the photos.

He raised the gun.

"The wall of shame," he said softly, just before pulling the trigger and shooting Nixon between the eyes.

Andy and I admired Dad as he expertly shot a few rounds at the four faces, chatting away and offering shooting tips until the pages were obliterated and nothing more than tattered remains; confetti from a victory parade; a statement of his wishes for the politicians' careers.

"Well, that's enough for tonight," Dad said, and packed his gun and supplies away.

We walked upstairs to the living room and I turned on the TV while Dad made us Denver omelets for dinner.

"What'd you think of the shooting?" I asked my brother later, as we sat on the floor watching *Tony Orlando and Dawn* and eating malted milk balls. "That was weird, huh."

"Yeah, weird but fun," Andy said. It *was* fun, and learning how to shoot a gun beat listening to Dad teach us how to weather-strip a drafty window or label a fuse box.

The bullet-riddled photos of the politicians stayed up for a year or two, like pieces of art in a strange, damp basement gallery.

Chapter Twenty-Eight

"I need to stop at the store on the way home," Dad said to me and my little brother as we drove down Holgate to 82nd. "You guys want a candy bar?"

Dad had just gotten off work at his real estate job and picked us up for our Wednesday night sleepover. He needed a few staples—chocolate milk and marshmallow cream (he drank both)—so we made what we thought would be a quick trip to the Fred Meyer on Johnson Creek Boulevard. We didn't get candy very often with Mom, but with Dad, it was a pretty regular thing. Another perk of the divorce. And Dad's pot smoking.

The three of us walked into the busy store, and I noticed the hustle and bustle, the after-work rush of mothers and fathers picking up items for dinner; the checkers announcing deli specials and requesting price checks over the loudspeaker. Dad and Andy and I headed to the candy section. *What will it be tonight?* I thought as I approached the shelves of goodies. *Mounds or Milky Way?* I checked out my choices, and spotted her: a little girl, dressed in ragged jeans and dirty tennies; her hands jammed in the pockets of her stretched-out, ill-fitting sweat jacket. A ragamuffin, rough around the edges.

I looked her up and down. Then I looked myself up and down. *I* was dressed in ragged jeans and dirty tennies. *I* had on an ill-fitting sweat jacket. *I* was rough around the edges. The only difference between me and this girl was that I had a parent with me. She looked to be unsupervised. I passed directly behind her as we looked at candy.

Dad was a purist and decided quickly: a Hershey bar and a bag of Kisses went into his hand-held basket. "Kids, I'm going to the next aisle over," he said. "Come get me when you're done."

"OK!" we said. Dad turned from us and rounded the corner to cookies, puffing on his pipe.

I debated a minute more, then grabbed a Mounds bar; Andy, a Butterfinger. I started to pull my brother up the aisle, but something made me pause. I stopped again to regard the little girl perusing the candy section, and glanced around for a corresponding adult. Still none. *Odd.* It was nighttime. Late in the fall, and raining. This girl was too young and it was too dark for her to be alone and presumably walking home on this busy section of 82nd Avenue. This particular Fred Meyer was surrounded by heavy traffic and businesses on all sides.

I held Andy by the coat sleeve and picked up a Big Hunk, pretending to browse. I side-stepped down the aisle, facing the shelves, but with an eye on the girl. What was she up to? A normal kid picking out a candy bar would be on a mission, scanning the shelves with a single goal in mind: getting one, paying for it, and ripping it open as soon as she got two feet away from the checkout counter. We weren't shopping for bridal gowns here. She stood and stood; unmoving, her hands shoved in the pockets of her jacket.

That's when I saw it, with my own two eyes—saw her take her right hand out of her pocket, pick up a candy bar, and put it in her pocket. Then she turned her attention back to the racks of candy bars, and stood some more.

I knew what was happening. She had no intention of paying for the candy.

She was stealing it.

A real live shoplifter! I'd never seen one before. And I could tell by her unease that this was probably a first for her, too. She didn't walk or run, or move at all. I'd never stolen anything, but I knew that after stealing, step two was *leaving*. Making for the doors.

I studied her. The thin brown hair grazing her shoulders; the faded jeans. I guessed her to be a fourth-grader, same as me, and I wondered how a person her age worked up the nerve to steal something from a store like Fred Meyer. Wasn't she afraid of getting caught? I wondered what kind of candy bar she was—

All of a sudden, she turned my way. I'd been caught! I was a witness! From fifteen feet away, my doppelganger looked hard into my eyes. Hers were mean, and they said, "You better not tell."

Dad!

I threw the Big Hunk down—I hated Big Hunks,

anyway—grabbed Andy by the scruff, and speed-walked around the corner to the next aisle.

Dad would know what to do. He was a disciplinarian from way back. With seven kids, disciplining was basically his job. Kind of his hobby, too. His natural fatherly tentacles extended to all kids: his own, the neighbors', kids of strangers. He scolded boys playing with matches; teenagers riding their bikes too fast on a strip mall sidewalk. Any child running with a stick. After Dad had gone to Raleigh Hills Clinic, he explained his alcoholism to me, saying his craving for alcohol had been a *deep tissue need.* I think he had that same issue when it came to busting kids. It was physiological. *In his tissues.*

I found him crouched amongst the Oreos and Archway Oatmeal Raisins.

"Dad," I whispered, "I saw a girl stealing a candy bar! I saw her do it! She's got a candy bar in her pocket!"

Dad put down whatever chocolate thing he had in his hands and stood ramrod-straight. *A kid stealing? Right here in the store?* He lived for this kind of crap. This was way better than scolding some trouble-maker hitting the crosswalk button just to make the traffic stop, or lecturing a few punk teenagers about using foul language at the ballpark. This one here had some meat on the bone. I discreetly pointed him three quarters of the way down the candy aisle to the girl: *still* standing there, *still* with her hands in her pockets.

Father assessed the scene. He stopped at the end of the aisle and checked out our young damsel; our adorable, unsupervised ragamuffin. He set his basket on the ground and readied himself, looking dapper and bald, and with lit pipe in hand he entered the aisle. "You kids stay here," he whispered. Andy and I stood our distance, peering around the corner of the end cap and let Kojak do his thing.

Dad walked slowly but purposefully down the aisle. He reached the candy bars and our girl, and paced behind her once, then twice. She fidgeted slightly, and the candy bar crinkled in her jacket pocket. Her eyes darted side-to-side. She sensed Dad, and looked like she may be having second thoughts about this caper, but she couldn't run now, not with some official-looking bald dude in a suit behind her.

Puffing on his pipe, his wing-tipped shoes *click-clicking* on the linoleum tiles, Dad approached our would-be thief. Blue-gray smoke billowed upwards in an ominous plume, and the dragnet closed in; he was practically breathing down the little girl's neck. He stopped a mere two feet behind her, removed his pipe and spoke clearly, sternly and deliberately to her tiny back:

"The only bad thing about being the store detective is you have to bust little kids stealing candy."

KA-ZOW!

The girl's eyes flew open. She reached deep into her jacket pocket, grabbed the candy bar, and with no regard to its landing point, flung it at the shelves full of goodies. It hit the racks and dropped to the ground. We watched the ragged jeans and scuffed tennies sprint down the aisle, toward the exit doors and out of our sight, like a bolt of lightning. The only remaining evidence: a slightly mangled Milky Way lying on the grocery store floor.

A girl after my own heart.

I fell on the floor.

Oh, Dad was pleased. He strolled toward me and Andy at the end of the aisle, puffing on his pipe, with a serious, satisfied expression. He might have just saved a little girl from a life of crime, or a trip to juvie. At the very least, a stern talking-to from the store manager.

He'd accomplished what he'd set out to do: scare some kid straight.

Chapter Twenty-Nine

"What say we take a drive?" Dad said to me and Andy as he backed the '48 out of the parking lot of the Plaid on Foster.

What say we don't, I thought, and looked over at my little brother and frowned. Now we understood why Dad had stopped at Plaid Pantry and gotten us each an Orange Crush. It was a payoff. A pre-payoff.

"Taking a drive" was Dad-code for traveling nine miles an hour up and down the streets of Portland in his weekend car, a 1948 Plymouth, participating in the most boring activity in history: looking at houses.

"And I've got a lady friend coming along," he told us as he rolled through a right turn at the intersection of 39th and Holgate. "We met at an open house. She's a real real estate buff."

A real estate buff? I glanced at Andy again. *Well, that's the best kind!* Nothing I'd rather do than sit in a hot car on a hot Sunday afternoon with newly-licensed real estate agents who got excited pointing out the value of a hedge.

Dad loved houses. He'd always enjoyed checking out beautiful homes, and now it was part of his job; he needed to stay current on the Portland housing market. He liked to beautify his own home, too, the house and the landscaping, and had made improvements at his new place on Sherrett Street. He'd recently remodeled the bathroom, and painted the dining and living rooms. Outside, he repaired his leaning porch, adding a handrail and fresh paint, and replaced his old front door with a decorative one made of solid oak. His new favorite phrases were "sweat equity" and "curb appeal", and on our weekends with him, he put me and Andy to work, usually in the yard. While he trimmed shrubs and laid brick walkways, he had me and my little brother pick up rotten apples that had fallen off the two trees in front.

Today, instead of picking up apples, we'd be "taking a drive." With "a lady friend."

There was Paulette. And Edie. There was a Linda.

This one was Barb.

Or was it Gloria? BarbGloria. The lady with the hair. A hybrid Carol Brady/Shirley Partridge do: a flipped, lacquered, immobile helmet, blond at the bottom and brown near the top. It was strange enough to see my dad with women who weren't my mom, but now this one had hair that was two colors.

Oh, BarbGloria was nice enough, friendly and younger than Dad, but they all were.

We drove to the Hawthorne area to pick her up for their second date, and found her waiting on her porch when we pulled up. She skipped down the steps and to the car in her beige pantsuit, and I was nearly blinded by her outfit's large square brass belt buckle reflecting the sun. This belt buckle could have been used to guide ships into port. Barb Gloria opened the door and flopped into the Plymouth's gigantic front seat, and immediately turned to me and Andy in the back. "Hi, kids!" she said, her face a wide-open smiling plate. She froze for a long few seconds as she took us in, her blue eyes sparkling, eyelids straining under the weight of a full pound of mascara and no less than five shades of sparkly shadow each. She smiled and smiled. I could see every single one of her teeth.

Finally, the staring contest ended (we won!) and she turned and gave Dad a playful tap on the shoulder and a scolding *tsk*, as if he'd held back in describing just how adorable we were. "Well, your dad told me you two were something," she said, turning to us and gazing again into our retinas, "and he was right!"

I looked sideways at Andy. We were something. *I knew it!*

Dad beamed.

As he pulled away from the curb, BarbGloria engaged me in conversation. She asked me how old I was and if I liked school. Adults always asked those questions. Did they really care how old I was or if I liked school? Was that interesting to them? Maybe it was. Adults seemed to like boring things.

Like looking at houses.

Dad got back on 39th and headed north. He crisscrossed over to the Hollywood district, then drove down busy NE Broadway where we entered historic Irvington, his favorite neighborhood, filled with large, stately homes on wide, tree-lined avenues. In Irvington, the streets became shady and cool due to the canopy of huge oak trees that blocked the sun—the entire tableau serene and lush and pic-turesque—great if you liked that sort of thing. We hit NE Brazee and inched along toward Knott Street.

"Just a gorgeous neighborhood," BarbGloria said, ad-miring the houses left and right.

"Yes, it is," Dad agreed. "One of the most desirable zip codes in Portland!" In addition to curb appeal and sweat equity, Dad mentioned zip codes a lot lately, too.

I leaned back and extended my legs. This gangster car sat fifteen people comfortably, and was so big my feet didn't even hit the couch-sized front seat. Andy and I could have a full-volume conversation, and Dad and BarbGloria wouldn't hear a thing. I took a drink of my Orange Crush and sank down low.

"Careful with the soda pops," Dad said as he looked in his rearview. He couldn't see us. "Take a look at that one," he said to Babs. "Nice low-maintenance front yard. Buyers like that."

"Ohhh, yes," she replied.

I turned to Andy. "Ohhhh, yes!" I whispered. I nod-ded like a toothless person in an old folks' home, and Andy crossed his eyes and made a face like a buck-toothed chip-munk. *Low-maintenance front yards are all the rage!*

Dad glanced again into his rearview. "What are the three most important things in real estate, kids? Location, location, location!" he bellowed, before Andy or I had a chance to answer. He was bonkers. Babs smiled and scooted to her left.

Am I in Hell? Maybe kids who are bad get sent to Hell and have to drive around with adults looking at houses.

Dad turned the corner at grandfather speed and started down another Irvington street, droning on about the value of original stained glass windows, new roofs, wraparound porches—and the *pièce de résistance*, the *crème de la crème*, the greatest thing ever invented: the corner lot!

"A corner lot adds about ten percent to the value of the home," Dad said.

"I did not know that," Babs purred as she rubbed Dad's neck.

Could we please head back now? I'd like to pick rotten apples out of the yard.

Dad and Babs were two peas in a real-estate-loving pod. Dad drove up Stanton and took a left on 17th Avenue, where Babs got into the act and started pointing at home after home in case Dad missed one as he slowed to three miles per hour. The old people who lived in this neighborhood were passing us by. On foot. In their walkers.

"Oh my God, Leon, look at that one!" Babs said as she pointed to a house. It was brown. She pointed to another. "Oh my God, look at that one!" It was tan. Was this a spiritual experience for her? It *was* Sunday; maybe she should have gone to church.

"Oh yeah, that one is nice," Dad said to Real Estate Barbie. "That's a creampuff. One level. Fully fenced. Excellent value."

It was official: the adults in this car were off their rockers. Who knows what might have happened if we'd passed a one-level home with a low-maintenance front yard and a newly installed thirty-year composite roof—on a corner lot! Dad might have had an accident.

Andy and I mocked Dad and BarbGloria from the backseat as we drove around for the next five hours and the two of them had real estate spaz attacks.

Chapter Thirty

Traffic on Weidler was heavy, moving slowly enough that Dad was able to point out the landmarks of his childhood, like he always did when we were near Lloyd Center Mall. "That office building there," he said, a Pall Mall between his fingers, "that whole block used to be nothing but a ball field. Frankie Schmidt and I used to smoke cigarettes in that field in the ninth grade." He put the cigarette in his mouth and loosened his tie.

Dad and I were in the Plymouth, heading east on Weidler, returning home after he'd run an errand off of Williams Avenue. We passed NE 11th Avenue, then 12th, and Dad pointed out another building, one he claimed had housed a bakery eighty years ago. "Me and Frankie used to get a piece of pie at a bakery there—Kaufmann's it was called—on Saturdays," he said. "For a *nickel*. After we'd gone to the movies. *Which cost a dime!*"

Dad was alternating between feeling nostalgic—this was the neighborhood he'd grown up in—*and* testy; it was about a hundred degrees out, and sitting in our un-air-conditioned car in this sea of idling automobiles, it felt ten degrees hotter.

How Dad had gotten caught in five o'clock rush hour traffic on a hot summer afternoon in this gritty, congested section of Northeast Portland, I didn't know. He usually avoided rush hour, traffic of any kind really, and naturally didn't like it when people got too close or tailgated, especially when he was driving the Plymouth. With its beautiful, curvaceous front bumpers and suicide doors, this Al Capone car was his pride and joy, even if it did still need some work.

"Watch it, buddy," Dad said to the driver next to us as he kept his place in the bumper-to-bumper traffic.

We inched along.

Dad pulled a folded handkerchief from the breast pocket of his shirt and wiped his forehead. The lanes began to narrow and the cars to our left were mere feet away. He looked over and muttered a curse word at the driver from a minute ago, a dude driving a white sedan.

"Well, if this guy thinks he can *mutter mutter mutter…*" Dad said. "Oh, now he's going to *mutter mutter mutter…?*"

Dad revved the motor and worked the shifter on the steering column, holding his ground in the barely-moving line. This was *his* turf. *His* old stomping grounds.

We continued up Weidler, stopping and starting, starting and stopping, doing a halting crawl along the busy four-lane boulevard. The smell of exhaust fumes wafted through the open windows, and Dad muttered again at the dude to our left.

"What does this guy think he's doing?" he said bitterly. I raised myself up in the giant front seat and looked past Dad's window, at the chugging cars and the wavy columns of heat. I saw the dude next to us, looking at Dad, then at the road in front of him. Back at Dad. The offending driver, beefy and much younger than Dad, yelled and gesticulated from behind the wheel of his grimy car, and Dad yelled and gesticulated back.

We came to a stop.

Suddenly, something triggered. *What happened?* I'd taken my eyes off the action to my left to look at the 7-Eleven on my right, but in an instant, the dude was out of his car, walking in front of it and toward us. Toward Dad. Hitching up his jeans by the belt loops and puffing up his chest. Striding fast and purposefully, and so mad, he had left his own car, parked and still running, in the middle of a busy Northeast Portland street!

I stretched my neck in order to see out the window. "What's he doing?" I said. Dad didn't answer, but I didn't expect him to, because at that moment, the dude was five steps away.

Then I saw it. Torso. Size Large. At the window. Like he was there to take our order.

Dad reacted. In one motion, he reached under his seat with his right hand and calmly pulled out a small handgun.

A gun! I didn't know my dad kept a gun in the car! Not since he'd had me and Andy shoot magazine photos of Richard Nixon and Spiro Agnew in the basement of his house on Sherrett Street had I seen him with a gun in his hand. Was this the same gun? *Why did he have a gun?!*

He placed it in his lap with the barrel facing toward the driver's door, and with his left hand, rolled up the window so that just a few inches' clearance remained.

I looked toward the window at the thick torso, the slight paunch hanging over the waistband of the jeans, and the muscular arms. I saw automobiles on all sides; heard the rumbling of engines and the occasional honking horn. I eyed the gun on Dad's lap.

Dad whispered to himself through clenched teeth— *Try it, you son of a bitch*—and lifted the pistol two inches off his lap.

The dude leaned down and toward the window, resting his hands on Dad's door. "Listen, you goddamn—"

He made eye contact—with Dad, then the gun—and straightened. Stepped back from the window. The chest un-puffed and the aggressive stance softened. The intimidating stare melted into a look of alarm. Confusion. Shock. Finally, comprehension.

Gun. Crazy bald man. Bulging veins on forehead. Retreat now!

The dude paused, then rotated his thick body slightly toward his vehicle. He blinked. Pondered. He took three steps to his car, and leaned down. What was he doing? Checking his tires?

Checking his tires.

He touched his front tire with his fingertips, as if re-moving a smudge. He rubbed another spot; maybe there was a bit of debris. And what was that? A pebble stuck in the tread?

The dude walked to the back of his car and did the same

to the rear tire. Wiped another smudge. Smoothed a scuff. Tightened the little rubber cap on the air nozzle thingy. The *Shrader valve*, it's called. I learned this from Dad. The dude's must have been loose.

Cars rumbled and idled on all sides.

He turned his back to us and walked calmly toward the front of his sedan, which sat smack in the middle of the long line of cars, and got back into the driver's seat. He put his dusty car back in gear and idled slowly forward, not looking Dad's way again. Dad un-tensed and did something to the gun, muttering more curse words as he carefully placed it back under his seat. He took a few deep breaths as he inched up Weidler, and we headed for home.

Whew. I slumped back down in the seat and looked over at Dad.

Bald man with a gun wins.

Violence deterred.

Chapter Thirty-One

I t had been ages since all seven of us had been on an outing with Dad. My older siblings were in high school now, and too busy to do much with parents. Mitzi was a senior, and Terri had a job and a serious boyfriend. Tony and Joe had started working, too.

But tonight, it would be just like the old days: seven kids crammed in a car—actually, a green, beat-up and mostly windowless van Dad had picked up to haul stuff around to his newly purchased rental properties.

Seven o'clock came, and we all jogged down the alley in our coats and gloves to meet Dad at the end of the block.

Tony opened the van's heavy sliding door with a clunk, and we piled into the back with Dad's landlording supplies: bags of tools and plastic paint buckets, rolls of remnant carpet.

"Hey, Dad," we said.

"Hey, kids," he said back, reaching behind his seat and moving stuff around to make room. I hopped up into the cargo area and found a plastic bucket for a seat. Dad had the heat cranked like an old person.

Tonight was a special occasion: we were going to see a movie—*Young Frankenstein*—with Dad and his new girlfriend, Laurel. I'd met Laurel a few times before, but this night would be the first time the nine of us would all be together; a test drive for what would probably be a new family unit.

I liked Laurel. She was nice and down-to-earth and closer in age to Dad than some of his previous girlfriends. She and Dad were a great match: for one thing, she knew how to handle his moods; and for another, she had two teenage daughters and wasn't interested in having any more kids. Dad had ended one serious relationship about a year ago over the baby thing. That was Helen. She was nice, too, but after dating Helen for more than a year, Dad told me and Andy we'd no longer be seeing her. "Helen wanted to have a baby," he'd said, "and I had to tell her I was done having babies."

There'd be no more babies for our family, but I was going to have two step-sisters, Leanne and Tia, and I wanted to meet them.

On the drive to Laurel's, Dad told us about Leanne, a tough girl who at age fifteen was the neighborhood foosball champ. "Leanne's a sweet girl, cute as a button," he said over his shoulder to no one in particular, "but she doesn't believe I have seven kids. When I talk about you guys, she says, 'You do not have seven kids!' and I tell her, 'Yes, I do!' She thinks

I'm kidding. Wait 'til she meets you all."

"Are we going to meet her tonight?" I asked.

"Not tonight," he said. Leanne and Tia weren't joining us for the movie. "Another time."

He pulled into Laurel's driveway, put the van in park and left the motor running. "I'll just be a few minutes. Want me to leave the radio on?"

"Yes!" I said.

"Seasons in the Sun" by Terry Jacks. I loved that song. Dad slammed his door with a clang and walked up the driveway to get Laurel.

My siblings and I sat in the warm van, six of us in the windowless cargo area, squatting on milk crates, flattened cardboard, whatever we could find. Joe sat in the passenger seat, manning the radio.

"You Ain't Seen Nothing Yet" by Bachman-Turner Overdrive.

"Turn it up," Tony said.

Joe turned it up.

We killed time and waited for Dad. I asked Terri to braid my hair, and positioned myself in front of her. Mitzi sat on her bottom, stretched her arms above her head and then touched her toes, doing quasi-yoga poses. The single dome light shone down onto the top of Andy's blond head as he pulled at fibers in the carpet.

Terri got to the end of my braid and I held my arm up over my head to hand her a ponytail holder. "Open the door!" I said. "It's too hot in here."

"No, it's too cold outside," Annie said. "Leave it closed."

"Open it, please!" I whined.

"Leave it closed!"

We left it closed. The van heated up. The lone window at the back of the cargo area steamed over. We waited.

Tony drummed on a plastic paint bucket. "You can turn it down now, Joe," he said. "Actually, turn it off. This song stinks."

"Muskrat Love" by America.

"No, leave it! I like this song," I said.

Suddenly the humongous, hundred-pound sliding side door opened with a *whooomp* and a *thud*, stopping hard at the end of its track.

Standing before us was a teenaged girl, dressed in jeans and a navy blue sweatshirt. A girl with long, shiny brown hair; a Valerie Bertinelli look-alike, if Valerie Bertinelli were playing the part of a 15-year-old problem child in an *ABC Afterschool Special*. One who smoked half a pack a day and had an issue with authority, in addition to beautiful skin and straight teeth.

We didn't know this girl.

Her eyes got big as she took us in, seven kids with identical noses and brows, sitting on overturned paint buckets and carpet logs. Touching each other's hair. Light shining from a single overhead dome, casting eerie down-shadows. A steamed rear window and a weird song about mating rodents playing softly in the background.

She stared, and we stared back. No one spoke or moved, and she didn't take her hand off the handle of the door. The motor rumbled and muskrats chirped.

"Oh. Shit," she said. She pulled on the handle and heaved the sliding door closed with a *thwack*.

My siblings and I looked at each other.

"That musta been Leanne," Joe said.

Chapter Thirty-Two

The sun was out and the highway was dry as we cruised down I-5 on a late summer road trip: Mom and the seven of us kids in the Old Gray Door, heading south to Medford, Roseburg, Chiloquin—some Southern Oregon town to visit one of our mother's thousand cousins.

We sped by miles of brown grass and Scotch broom while American kids in American cars hung their arms out windows and stared at their fellow travelers because there was absolutely nothing else to do.

Perfect.

We got ready.

Joe sat in the backseat and grabbed the tape dispenser he'd packed along with his comics and deck of cards. He pulled off a piece of tape for himself, then handed the dispenser my way. I took a piece, and gave the roll to Andy, who had a window. Our littlest brother was prone to carsickness and needed easy access.

Joe looked behind him at the stream of cars on the highway. "Get ready!" he said as he attached his tape. "Bunch of cars coming up in the fast lane!"

Tony sat in the front with Annie and Mom, his elbow hanging out the passenger window. He turned around. "Give it here when you're done," he said, and Andy slammed the tape dispenser into his extended hand. Tony cut a strip for himself and handed the tape to Annie, who struggled with her piece.

"I'm too sweaty, it won't stick!" she said as she raised herself off her seat, grabbed the rearview mirror and pointed it her way.

"Sit down, please," Mom said.

"You need to dry your forehead off," Joe said, "then stick it on at the last second."

"It won't stick!"

"I need a longer piece," Andy said from the back.

"Well, get one," Joe replied. Tony grabbed the tape off the front seat and tossed it to Andy in the back.

Mitzi sat next to me with a pad and pencil, speed-sketching her art gallery-worthy pieces—a passing truck stop sign, a close-up of the door handle—while Terri sat at the window behind Mom with a bag of yarn and her crochet project. Mitzi and Terri each dropped what they were working on and took a piece of tape.

"Got it!" Annie said to her reflection, finally getting the tape to stick.

"I guess I need a piece, too," Mom said as she drove.

"Gotta make it believable."

* * *

Taping up our noses: a gloriously twisted highlight of our summer road trips. Joe had come up with this stunt one night as he walked to the dinner table, normal as you please, but with the tip of his nose pulled straight up and held with a piece of tape he'd attached to his forehead. He sat down at the dining room table and placed his paper napkin politely in his lap. He dished up and took a bite of his mashed potatoes, but wasn't able to close his mouth all the way, resulting in a smacking noise.

"Please don't chew with your—" Mom said. "Oh, Gads. What in the world are you doing?"

We all stopped, mid-chew, and stared at Joe. His nostrils were near vertical. His upper lip curled back grotesquely, unnaturally; so much so, I could see that little piece of connecting tissue above his front teeth as he tried to eat. He looked ghastly: part human, part pig, part buck-toothed cartoon bunny rabbit. Disgusting and awesome.

* * *

As unsuspecting travelers approached, we got ready. With one piece of tape each, we'd transformed ourselves into a car full of pig people.

I leaned over Mitzi and poked Andy in the leg to get his attention. I exaggerated my breathing for effect. We snorted at each other like asthmatic sows. Crossed our eyes like mutant basement-dwellers. I looked at Mom, and admired her piggy profile; especially awful. We were a traveling freak show in an unwashed black Buick LeSabre, one with a primer-gray driver's side door and a loose muffler. The highway hummed beneath our wheels, and we put the windows up, creating just the right amount of glare to hide the shine of the tape. "White station wagon!" Joe hollered, identifying our target car.

I stood up in the backseat, my head nearly grazing the ceiling of the car, to get one last look at myself in the rearview. (*Gross. Yes!*) Andy did the same.

"Sit down, please!" Mom said. But we just snorted. It's hard to take your mom seriously when she looks like Porky Pig.

"On three!" Joe said.

Our victims approached.

"One." We sat motionless and looked straight ahead, straight-faced. And pig-nosed. Mom drove, eyes on the road.

"Two. Nobody move."

Mom adjusted her speed, keeping pace with the white wagon in the lane to her left. She sped up, slowed down, then held Old Gray steady with the car carrying a family of five. A family that probably played Slug Bug or the license plate game on road trips. A family that was probably normal.

We were neck-and-neck, traveling the same speed. I could sense the family looking at us, this car stuffed full of people just feet away.

"Three!" Joe said.

In one synchronized move, the eight of us turned our heads abruptly to the left and stared, expressionless.

The kids in the wagon started at our eight heads turning in unison. They gawked at our open, gummy mouths. Our pig noses. The girl in the backseat did a double-take, and her eyes bulged. Through the slight glare of our windows, what was she seeing? A bunch of hideous, pig-nosed kids, even a pig-nosed mom! She turned her face slowly forward so as not to appear rude, but her eyes wouldn't obey. They were locked on us, and she stared some more. Her big brother next to her burst out laughing. He smacked the shoulder of a sibling next to him, and did the same to a parent in the front seat. He pointed, shamelessly, and laughed harder. The little brother looked at us, confused. The mother turned our way and gaped. I saw her lips move. "Now, it's not nice to stare…" I imagined her saying. "*Good God, what's wrong with those people?*" She couldn't help but laugh. The father glanced over, shook his head, and smiled.

Mom drove alongside the wagon for a good five seconds, allowing the family in the wagon to feast their eyes on our snouty, squirrelly, rat-pig faces. The fishbowl of freaks in the black car with the primered door.

What *were* we?

We were hideous.

Mom slowed down and let the white wagon pull ahead, and we all watched the kids in the backseat crane their necks for one last look as they cruised on down the Interstate. Mom pulled the tape off her nose and glanced at the five of us in the backseat, falling over each other in laughter. Annie slid down in the front seat, bicycle-kicking her legs in glee, and next to her, Tony looked out the window, threw his head back and cracked up.

We pulled our tape off and got ready for our next victims.

Acknowledgments

I'd like to thank everyone who read or critiqued this book, or any excerpt or portion of. A special thank you to those patient people who gave me feedback on my early drafts: Jill Kaady Gilbertson, Tim DeMartino, Laura Campbell, Leo Baldwin, Tom Reynolds, Paula Reynolds Snoddy, Anne Lieder, and Ray Johnston. Each and every one of you, thank you!

Thanks to all who donated to my Kickstarter!

To Mitzi, Terri, Tony, Joe, Annie and Andy. I love you. Thanks for all the material.

To Mom and Dad, for doing what you did. My childhood was amazing, and I wouldn't change a thing.

To my editor John Hart for his excellent work. To Bryan Tomasovich at The Publishing World, for the marketing guidance and expertise. To Leslie Calderoni, for the script doctoring.

To all my friends and extended family for the encouragement.

To my daughters, Evin and Angela, for their patience and pep-talks. (Especially Angie for the pep-talks.)

To Ron, for listening. Over and over and over.

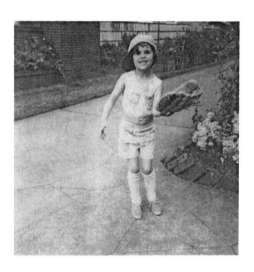

Let's hear it for the rhythm method! Standing, from left:
Joe, Tony, Mitzi, and Terri. Seated from left: Sherri,
Andy (in Mom's lap), and Annie.

Front cover design: Joe Bobzien

UFO painting, back cover: Tony Bobzien

Raking Leaves painting: Tony Bobzien

Author photograph: Mark O Rogers

visit www.sherribobzien.com

CPSIA information can be obtained
at www.ICGtesting.com
Printed in the USA
FSOW01n2019231015
12552FS

9 781634 136006